You & Heaven
by
David Gabriel

Blue Zoo
England

Copyright © David Gabriel 2023

All rights reserved. No part of this work may be reproduced, stored in a retrieval system, or transmitted in any form or by any means — electronic, mechanical, photocopying, recording or otherwise — without the prior permission of the publishers.

Disclaimer: The publisher and the author make no representations or warranties with respect to the accuracy or completeness of the contents of this work and specifically disclaim all warranties, including without limitation warranties of fitness for a particular purpose. The information presented is to be used for informational and entertainment purposes only and being the author's opinion, does not constitute any form of professional advice. The advice and strategies contained herein may not be suitable for every person and every situation. Neither the publisher nor the author shall be liable for damages arising herefrom.

Published by Blue Zoo, Yorkshire, England.

You & Heaven

The Proof We All Crave   7

Discover What You Are Looking For   13

Making the Complex Easy   16

Does The Afterlife Exist?   22

What is the Soul?   33

What - and When - is the Afterlife?   46

Meeting Departed Loved Ones   67

Reliving the Best of Times   75

The Best Version of You   82

Animals, Friends, and Everything in the Afterlife   88

An Average Day in the Afterlife   101

My Gift   117

Questions about Heaven   119

For those who stood at my shoulder
guiding my hand
as I wrote this book.

The Proof We All Crave

You're going to find answers in this book. Answers to every question you've ever asked about the afterlife. But I guarantee they won't be the answers you are expecting because what awaits you is so much more than you could ever imagine.

You see, when we picture the afterlife, we typically envision an idealized version of heaven that we've taken from a book or movie. It's beautiful, and perfect, but it's vastly oversimplified and hugely impractical. There's rarely any actual detail of how the afterlife works, what we do there, and importantly, how it's possible to do it all. It's like looking at an unknown fruit in a photograph and trying to imagine what eating it is like. We can guess, but without extra information, we have no idea. The taste could be sweet or sour, while the texture could be crunchy like an apple or squishy like a grape. It's the same problem with the afterlife — we have too little information.

So, how can we see the bigger picture?

In this book, I'll be painting a detailed picture of the afterlife, so you can discover exactly what is waiting for you. A picture that will absolutely stun you. Not by its beauty, though it goes without saying that the afterlife is breathtaking, but by the opportunities it will afford you that you have probably never dreamed possible.

Chapter by chapter, we'll build up this picture so that everything will easily slot into place as the wonders are revealed one by one. Wonders you'll encounter in no other book, course, documentary, or seminar.

That's a bold claim, so let's have a sneak peak at what we're going to explore together:

> how you can live out your dreams in the afterlife and what you need to know to be able to do that

> how you can watch over the loved ones you've left behind *and* spend time with those already departed *at the same time*

> how time doesn't work the way you believe it does and the secrets this unlocks for the afterlife, for example, being able to relive highlights from your past — the birth of a child, meeting your life partner, achieving an important milestone...

> and much, much more

If you come to this book with an open mind, it will unveil all the answers you are seeking. In detail. In plain language. In easy-to-grasp chapters. However, there's one thing it can't give you, which we have to establish right from the start because no book, person, or religion can provide it either: proof.

You see, with our current levels of knowledge and technology, it is impossible to produce proof. Of course we have faith, anecdotes, and plenty of wishful thinking, but no matter how much we want them to be, none of those are irrefutable proof.

As for science...

There are scientific discoveries that suggest the universe is very different from how we have perceived it to be for centuries, some of which will be useful in our exploration. But science has no actual proof, either.

You see, no matter how you look at it — using religion, reasoned argument, or science — producing proof is impossible. Not that we should be surprised by that when you consider the elusive nature of the afterlife and the complex questions we ask.

"What will happen to me when I die?"

"Do animals go to heaven?"

"Will I be reunited with my loved ones?"

We've all asked such things, but the problem is, we usually never find answers, only more questions.

Yet that shouldn't come as any surprise.

Over 2,300 years ago, Plato and Aristotle, two of the greatest minds of their age, debated the existence of life after death and the soul. We know they did because they left behind texts detailing their complex exchanges on these subjects, many of which are still studied in universities around the globe today. This debate happened so long ago, mathematics and science were in their infancy, while the world's largest religions were yet to emerge — Christianity (first century) and Islam (seventh century). Because of this, people were extremely limited in what resources they could draw upon to resolve their issues, so it wasn't unusual for them to turn to superstition, myth, and ancient deities. It's no surprise, then, that Plato and Aristotle found no conclusive answers.

Today, despite all of our wondrous advances, we are still struggling to answer those same questions. This subject is so complex and the opinions on it are so diverse, it's no wonder nothing has been resolved despite the passing of two millennia.

Yet those questions were asked long before Plato and

Aristotle contemplated them. Language evolved around 150,000 years ago. Obviously, the first talk was of food, shelter, danger, and procreation, but you can bet it wasn't long before conversations revolved around members of their fallen tribe and what had become of them.

So, potentially, we've had over 100,000 years of posing questions and yet, we don't have a single definitive answer to show for it.

But while proof is impossible, there is something that's almost as good.

Evidence.

In everyday life, people often use the words "evidence" and "proof" interchangeably, but they are very different animals.

Proof is conclusive validation that a particular proposition is true or false, or — possibly more appropriate for our needs — that a thing exists or doesn't exist.

Evidence, on the other hand, is one or more pieces of information that merely *suggest* a thing is true or false, or that it exists or doesn't exist. By amassing evidence in sufficient quantity and quality, it is often possible to establish proof, but each piece of evidence is only a starting point, not proof in itself. As such, the more evidence collected, the more likely is a definitive outcome.

This is why the prosecution in a criminal trial won't rely solely on, say, a single fingerprint from the crime scene to make their case but will introduce witness testimonies, DNA samples, CCTV footage, motives, and the like. Each piece of the puzzle builds to form a complete picture — the proof of the perpetrator of the crime. And this is exactly what we'll be doing — piecing the puzzle together using evidence and insights from all manner of sources and disciplines.

But a word of caution here — don't get hung up on trying to prove the existence of the afterlife. We can't do that. No one can. However, although only a small amount of evidence does not confirm that a thing is true or false, the existence of such evidence is crucial — by existing, that evidence confirms that there is the *possibility* that a thing *could* be true or false, and is therefore worthy of further consideration. For an exploration like ours, this is extremely important.

So, if you have an open mind, and the will to find answers, it is possible to paint a clear picture of what awaits us when we die. And to gain great comfort from that, which I'm guessing is one of the things you're looking for — it's amazingly freeing to know that death is not something to fear.

To that end, I'll be providing as much evidence as I can to support everything I'll be sharing with you. This will allow you to see for yourself that the view of the afterlife presented here is the most believable, logical, and well structured ever revealed.

The evidence will be presented in a variety of ways, each designed to make it easily digestible, and comes from a lifetime spent seeking answers to life's most perplexing mysteries. As I've traveled the world, I've encountered some fascinating people, many who shared their great wisdom on life and beyond — for example, a Buddhist monk, a Christian bishop, an African shaman... I've also had family members who were mediums, able to communicate with those who've passed on, and I've met people who have had a near-death experience which allowed them to see what lies beyond. What all of these people shared with me proved immensely enlightening, especially as some elements illuminated others, so could be built upon to form a cohesive whole.

This wealth of knowledge, combined with a love of logic and solving puzzles, has enabled me to formulate insights that will reveal everything you've always wanted to know about heaven, life after death, and the soul — about your "life" in the afterlife. In the coming chapters, we'll explore:

> what the afterlife actually is and how it works

> how time functions if the afterlife lasts for eternity

> how you can be with loved ones who have already passed

> how you can watch over your loved ones who are still on earth

> how revisiting cherished moments from your life is possible

> how you can explore the entire world

> how you can witness the whole of history

> how you can achieve goals you never dreamed possible

> and, crucially, how you can do as many of these things as you like *all at the very same time*

I hope you enjoy reading my book and find it provides the answers, and the comfort, you are seeking.

So, let's find some answers, shall we?

To put your mind at ease, you can expect no jargon, no filler, no fluff. Just straight talk, in plain English, that will give you a clear picture of everything you've been craving to know.

Oh, and no religious talk — I'm not looking to convert you, but to inform, reassure, and uplift you.

Discover What You Are Looking For

Most people have wondered about what comes after the life they're living now and, if there is something else, what it is. Surprisingly, while most contemplate this, very few take the time to visualize any of the details of what they might find in an afterlife. We're going to change that right now.

For a few minutes, read through the following questions — they're multiple choice, so it's easy — and consider what you picture the afterlife to be in a little more detail.

To keep it easy, there are only six questions, though there could have been many more. If you so wish, please treat the multiple-choice answers as jumping-off points, ideas to kick-start your mind into conjuring your own unique answers.

Don't worry, you won't be graded!

This quiz is purely so that, if you haven't already, you discover your reasons for wanting there to be an afterlife and what you expect out of one. As such, you don't need to remember your answers, but you do need to answer each question to get things clear in your own mind.

1. *What kind of a form will you have in the afterlife?*
A. I'll keep the body I have at the time of my death.

B. I'll exist as a being made of energy such as light.
C. I'll be incorporeal, kind of ghostlike.
D. I'll have the body I had in my prime, only better.
E. I'll be an angel.

2. How old will you be in the afterlife?
A I'll be young, fit, and healthy again, so maybe in my twenties.
B. I'll be ageless because I won't have a physical form and the spirit doesn't age.
C. I'll remain the age I was when I died.
D. I'll be any age I want to be.
E. I'll be the age from the happiest period of my life.

3. In what kind of space will you exist in the afterlife?
A. I'll live in a mansion in a luxury resort in a fabulous landscape where my every whim is catered for instantly.
B. I won't have a body, so I'll float among the clouds or merge with the universe in a great wave of bliss.
C. I'll live somewhere similar to the Garden of Eden, where I'm one with all things.
D. I'll live in a replica of my favorite home from my time on earth.
E. I'll exist like a molecule of water floating in an ocean of souls.

4. Will you have needs in the afterlife, such as the need to eat?
A. I won't "need" to do things such as eat, but I'll partake because I enjoy the experience.
B. I won't need sustenance because I won't have a physical form.

C. I'll need nourishment, rest, and shelter, even in the afterlife.
D. I'll be sustained by the love of those around me.
E. God will see that I get anything I need.

5. How will you spend your time in the afterlife?
A. I'll spend it with the loved ones I've lost.
B. I'll bask in God's love.
C. I'll watch over my family who are still on earth.
D. I'll search for answers to the mysteries it was impossible to explore while living.
E. I'll do all the things I never had the chance to do on earth.

6. What is your one reason, above all others, for wanting the afterlife to be real?
A. I want to be reunited with my loved ones.
B. I want to live forever.
C. I want to experience the happiness I never had in life.
D. I want to serve God.
E. I'm frightened of death, especially if it's drawn-out and painful.

You should now have a much clearer picture of what you are hoping for from the afterlife - what you'll look like, where you'll live, what you want to do there, everything. This will help you grasp the concepts we're going to explore and appreciate that the afterlife you've imagined is only the tip of the iceberg. There is so much more waiting for you!

Making the Complex Easy

In the coming chapters, we're going to dig deep into everything concerning the afterlife, which, obviously, means we are going to be considering some incredibly complex subjects. To be able to share the insights I have with you so that you can grasp them easily, I'll be drawing on some scientific principles, logic-based arguments, and research from a variety of disciplines.

Don't panic! If the terms "science," "logic," and "research" sound daunting, any such concepts will be broken down into the simplest of forms so you can understand what I'm saying without any head-scratching. Promise!

But that poses a problem.

While these strategies will enable you to quickly and easily grasp what I share, they come at a price, not least because I'll be using simple, everyday language. So no technical jargon, no archaic vocabulary, and no explanations so convoluted you need a PhD to understand what the devil I'm talking about. After all, you're here to uncover the secrets of life, death, and the universe, not to expand your English vocabulary in preparation for a spelling bee!

So simplicity is the key. The price of making things simple is that it will involve some inventive ways of breaking down complex concepts. I'm sure most readers will prefer simplicity over jargon-heavy babble, so to achieve this, I'll be giving lots of analogies, some of which might seem quite fanciful but which will get the points over wonderfully.

What do I mean by fanciful analogies?

Let me give you an example. Picture what I describe here:

It's a mammal. Big. Vegetarian. Four short legs and a stubby tail. It has small ears and eyes, but a big mouth. It's fat and gray-skinned. Or it looks fat, but in reality, it's just barrel-shaped.

Well? What animal is it?

Can you see a specific creature or only a vague blob?

If you said hippopotamus, bravo! But if not, don't worry about it, because that's kind of the point.

You see, such a description gives you a vague idea of the thing I'm talking about but leaves you to build it piece by piece in your mind. Which can be a problem if you don't grasp all the parts straight off the bat. For example, if you miss one of the important elements, which would be easy to do when so much info is blasted at you in no discernible order, what you'd end up with would be very different from what you were supposed to end up with. For instance, imagine if you missed the "gray-skinned" detail and so, with no information on its outer covering, you covered the animal in your mind in a fluffy fleece — that's not a hippo; that's a sheep.

Luckily, it gets much easier if we mix things up by looking at the problem another way.

How about if I said, "Picture a rhino, but with no horn and a bigger, wider mouth."

Can you see a hippo now? You can, can't you? That time, it jumped straight into your head without you even trying.

You see, that's much easier to picture because you've got a concrete image that only needs a few tweaks, as opposed to a ton of words that you have to fit together in a mental jigsaw puzzle.

Now, there's a big difference between a hippo and a rhino — the number of toes, size of their teeth, gestation periods, and the like. However, as is clear, the twelve words of the "rhino" sentence say far, far more than all of the information in the first description that has three times as many words. You see, it isn't the amount of information that matters, but the quality.

Because of this, so you can quickly and easily grasp all the concepts I'm going to share with you, I'll be illustrating some points using similar principles, with some truly out-of-the-box thinking.

Why out of the box?

There's a famous quote by German philosopher Ludwig Wittgenstein: "Whereof one cannot speak, thereof one must be silent."

Many people take that to mean that if someone doesn't know what they're talking about, then they shouldn't talk about that subject. Armed with this as a clever riposte, or a more modern version of it, people quote it, believing it's a way to silence someone who is blathering on about something they obviously know little about.

However, this is a misinterpretation.

What Wittgenstein is actually talking about is how language can sometimes let us down by not giving us the words we need to understand a subject enough to express our thoughts. I don't mean when there's a word on the tip of your tongue or when you struggle to explain something you've done or seen. What this quote is referring to is our inability to describe some part of the universe and reality clearly because the words simply do no exist to express such concepts.

Think of music or food. How often does someone ask you what a band is like or what a meal tastes like and you reply, "It's kind of like..."? It doesn't matter what comes next, what matters is literally the "kind of" — you don't have precise words to express your thought, so you have to grasp for things that are similar in the hope that the other person can piece a puzzle together that you're creating on the fly and thus understand what you mean.

Talking about huge subjects like the afterlife and the soul is like that — grasping at things that might "kind of" illustrate the point in the hope that it will enable someone else to piece the puzzle together.

But the issue doesn't stop there.

It's extremely difficult to convey complex concepts if you don't have the information in an easy-to-understand format. But what happens if you don't have the information in any format? What if the information is so abstract that words haven't even been invented to describe the things you want to discuss?

For example, think of something yellow.

On reading that, I bet you immediately saw images of yellow things in your mind whether you wanted to or not — a daffodil, the sun, butter...

But what if the word *yellow* had never been invented because we had no evidence that anything yellow existed?

We haven't invented a word for literally everything because that's impossible — we don't know what we don't know to be able to invent words for things it's impossible to predict the existence of.

When we don't have the correct words to describe something, we struggle to make our ideas solid for ourselves, let alone other people. This is a major problem when discussing the afterlife and the soul.

But even if we have the words, that doesn't necessarily mean explaining something will be easy. For example, imagine trying to describe, in as few words as possible, hiccups to someone who's never suffered them. See what I mean?

How we picture the universe, and beyond, is limited not only by our knowledge but also by our language. If we can't express an idea, how can we truly know anything about it? It escapes meaningful expression. Which is extremely puzzling and frustrating because it means we can know about something but be unable to talk about it. You see, language is a tool, and like all tools, it is limited in what it can achieve. Sometimes, it's like using a hammer when what you really need is a leaf blower.

As an example of the limitations language sometimes imposes on us, Germans have a word for the pleasure to be derived from someone else's failure — *schadenfreude*. English has no single-word equivalent, so instead we have to produce a whole sentence to explain what it means.

So this is why there will be some out-of-the-box thinking. And a liberal sprinkling of "rhino" illustrations.

But don't worry, because it's not all gray areas and problematic concepts. Some of what we're going to discuss will be backed by hard evidence from respected scientists and researchers. Some of this will be cutting-edge research; some will have been established for decades, the global scientific community having deemed it fact.

To that end, I will be drawing upon various disciplines to help us understand what awaits us after this life, including:

> physics
> astrophysics
> quantum mechanics
> biology
> neuroscience
> psychology
> logic

With regard to the cutting-edge research, this does not mean it is "research" that is so far beyond the fringes of science that it can no longer be classed as "proper" science. This is *real* science, conducted by respected scientists. Science so advanced, it is shaking the pillars of what we once believed about reality and how the universe works. Believe me, it's going to make you question a lot of your long-held beliefs. But in a good way! Such concepts will be presented to show you there are viable alternatives to how we traditionally perceive the universe and everything in it.

So, if you have an open mind and you are willing to view life, our world, and the universe in ways you never thought possible, I have wonders to share with you. First, we'll lay some groundwork so that the revelations to come will be easy to grasp, and then we'll dive into the afterlife to explore what it is and what we do there.

Let's get cracking.

Does The Afterlife Exist?

You're reading this book, so I'm guessing you already believe the afterlife exists, or at least believe in the possibility that it does. So if that's the case, why bother answering this question? Two reasons.

Firstly, because at some point in your life, you might wish to prove to a nonbeliever that the existence of the afterlife is a very real possibility. This chapter should give you the means to do that.

Secondly, for our own sakes, we need to establish a solid foundation upon which we can build our entire view of the afterlife; therefore, establishing the possibility of its existence is paramount.

Once we've done this, we can get into the nitty-gritty of what the afterlife actually is, how it functions, and how the soul can interact with it. And believe me, these concepts are going to amaze you!

So, is there really a heaven?

That's a simple question. You'd imagine there'd be a simple answer, wouldn't you? Especially when people have been searching for it for millennia. Literally.

But it's not surprising that such a massive question has never been answered. There are lots of arguments on both sides, but to date, nothing has ever been proven to resolve the matter one way or the other.

Considering how advanced we like to believe we are, that's kind of surprising. Surely with all our technology and great minds, we can uncover the truth.

If only it was that easy.

For centuries, science has struggled to disprove the existence of the afterlife or the soul. However, with such things seen as supernatural, many scientists have little time for them, instead preferring to use only hard evidence and solid facts to build their world. Especially as searching for such answers could be construed by some of their peers as crackpot science, thus tarnishing their reputations. Facing such pressures, it's no wonder that many scientists are so dismissive of the subject.

However, that is changing. It used to be that only philosophers, theologians, and mystics dared to investigate the afterlife, but nowadays, more and more researchers from other disciplines — even the hard sciences — are becoming interested. You see, personal belief systems aside, there appears to be a degree of convergence that is surprising many researchers and drawing them into the investigation.

Yet, despite the world's greatest minds pushing the boundaries of knowledge throughout history, every single one of them has failed to prove that the afterlife or the soul does not exist. Many scientists and laypersons alike do not believe in such because they claim that there is no evidence. Further, they often deride those who do believe, looking at them disdainfully as if they lack the intellect to grasp what is so blindingly obvious to anyone with half a brain.

Blindingly obvious?

Here's the thing about science — it *relies* on scientists constantly getting things wrong. Yes, you read that correctly — wrong.

Think about that. Because essentially, that's how science works. In fact, that's the only way science *can* work.

Let me explain. History's greatest minds once held as fact that the world was flat — they were wrong.

Later, other "great minds" maintained that the smallest thing in creation was the atom — they were wrong.

Later still, more "great minds" claimed that the area in which our solar system resides, the galaxy called the Milky Way, was the entire universe — they were wrong.

More recently, other "great minds" still stated categorically that nothing existed outside of our universe — they were...

Well, the jury is still out on that one. But you don't have to be a genius to see the number of times science's greatest minds were wrong and had to do a U-turn.

When the idea that our universe was only one of many was first voiced, it was laughed at as nonsense. However, today, many leading minds across different disciplines purport that there are multiple universes all existing simultaneously (a "multiverse"), while other equally respected people disagree, saying ours is the one and only universe. The simple truth is that we don't know.

The point is that the idea of a multiverse was once preposterous, but as we grow and evolve our knowledge, more and more "great minds" are starting to believe in the existence of parallel worlds where there is another "you" and another "me" — another everyone and everything — where history plays out differently because somewhere along the line, different choices were made to those "we" made "here."

You've probably come across this concept without even knowing it. Have you ever read Charles Dickens's *A Christmas Carol* or seen one of the Christmas movies about Ebeneezer Scrooge? In that story, Scrooge is visited by a number of ghosts that show him visions of his life, one showing him how the future will play out if he doesn't do something to change it — i.e., there are two alternative futures possible, one of which ends with him dying alone, unloved, and with no one to mourn his passing, while the other ends in a good old happily-ever-after style. In essence, this shows Scrooge having two distinct futures, each of which hinging on the decisions he makes. These futures can be thought of as two alternate realities or two universes — a tiny multiverse.

If you haven't come across this concept of a multiverse before, it can be quite daunting to get a handle on it at first, but it is really straightforward. In one alternate universe to ours, your life plays out pretty much exactly as it does here, but for one tiny instance where you made a different decision from the one you made here; in another universe, your life couldn't be more different because the different choices go right back to before your birth, so you're born into an entirely different universe to begin with.

For example, in our universe, you have a black puppy from a litter your neighbor's dog had. In the first alternate universe, you made one tiny decision that was different — you got a black-and-white puppy, the brother of the black one — but other than that, your lives pretty much run in parallel. In a third universe, where things are radically different because different decisions were made before you were even conceived, your father is the president of the United States (but don't get bigheaded because in a fourth, he's a serial killer!). See how it works? And there could be an infinite number of these alternate universes, so, literally, any scenario could be played out somewhere.

I love this idea. And I'm not the only one. There's a great movie from 1998 called *Sliding Doors*, written and directed by Peter Howitt (British readers might remember him as Joey in the TV comedy *Bread*). It stars Gwyneth Paltrow as she negotiates two parallel worlds, one in which she catches a particular train, the other in which she doesn't — that's the initial different element upon which everything else hinges. The story reveals the two very different outcomes from such a seemingly inconsequential event. It's well worth watching, not just because we're talking about this subject, but because it's simply a good movie.

Movie critiquing out of the way, don't get fixated on this concept of a multiverse. Though we'll double back to it at some point, it's only one small element of our exploration of the afterlife.

In the meantime, here's how science works, which is important to grasp because it has a bearing on how we often judge a thing's validity.

It's been said that scientists often don't prove a scientific theory but instead fail to disprove it. And that's a very important statement. After constantly failing to disprove something through rigorous observations and experiments, they often have no choice but to accept it as the best explanation — at that moment in history — for how or why the universe works as it does.

Remember when you were a kid learning to paint at school and you mixed blue paint with yellow paint and were amazed when it produced green? What did you do then? Experimented by mixing other colors, right?

Sometimes they produced a yucky mess, but other times, if you got the proportions correct, they created something pleasing. Slowly, you figured out — through trial and error — how colors worked.

At its core, that's what scientists do — they experiment, often resulting in something yucky, i.e., wrong, but occasionally producing something pleasing, i.e., right. They can set out to prove that one outcome happens when certain events occur, such as mixing two paints to get a specific color, or they can set out to disprove an outcome, such as dropping a penny off the top of the Empire State Building to see if it kills someone (which it doesn't — it's an urban myth that it could). Scientists must run such experiments over and over and over until they are certain the outcome will always be the same, at which point, the theory they're testing can reliably be said to be accepted or unaccepted (which, to the layperson, means proved or disproved).

This means that a heck of a lot of a scientist's time is spent failing. Depending on the complexity of the theory they are testing, they could continually fail for minutes, months, years, or even decades. That's a lot of failure! Not that they have any choice — constant failure isn't just a part of their job but fundamental to it because without it, they wouldn't be able to judge the validity of their hypotheses.

This goes some way to explaining why, to some laypersons, scientists appear a skeptical bunch of people who love nothing better than being awkward for the sake of it and so can't be wholly trusted. That's kind of understandable because scientists accept constant failure as part of life, whereas we, the laypeople, see failure as something to avoid at all costs, being interested only in success.

That's an uncomfortable juxtaposition. Especially as it isn't only scientists who grow through failure — we all do because we learn from our mistakes, i.e., our failures. You see, we are all "scientists" in our own ways, running experiments and acting on the results. Which is good, because we need proper scientists. Most importantly, we need their help if we're ever to prove, beyond a doubt, that the afterlife is real. We can't do that with faith, anecdotal evidence, or wishful thinking alone.

What does all of this have to do with the afterlife and proving it exists?

Let's see.

We've already discussed that science can't disprove the afterlife, but that fact has far-reaching consequences that actually do quite the reverse of what skeptics would like.

You see, instead of science proving the afterlife does not exist, it might actually prove it does!

You don't have to be a physics nerd to have heard of Schrödinger's cat. It's such a "fun" concept that it's entered popular culture by being used in more TV shows than I can remember, including *The Big Bang Theory, Silicon Valley, Stargate SG-1, Person of Interest, Doctor Who...*

If you haven't seen any of those, or read any of the novels that feature it (by authors such as Neil Gaiman, Terry Pratchett, Robert A. Heinlein, Douglas Adams...), here it is in a nutshell.

In 1935 two people were having a casual chat, as people do. Except these were two of the "great minds" of the time: Albert Einstein and Erwin Schrödinger. I'll break it down into steps to make it easier to digest. (And it's all theoretical, so no animals were harmed.)

Step 1

A cat is locked in a box for sixty minutes. You cannot see into this box or hear anything from inside it.

Step 2

Also inside the box is a device containing radiation, a Geiger counter, and a flask of poison. The device might or might not release this radiation at any moment during this sixty minutes of imprisonment. If it does, the Geiger counter will register it and the poison will be released, killing the cat.

Step 3

Because releasing the radiation is random — it might happen or it might not — at any time during the experiment, you have no idea if it has been released and the poison has killed the cat or if the cat is still alive because the device hasn't been activated.

Step 4

After the hour is up, you can open the box, which will reveal the fate of the cat.

Step 5

Here's the important part — until you open the box, it is impossible to know if the cat is alive or dead, so during that hour, the cat is both alive and dead at the same time. It's a cunning physics conundrum.

If that theory worked for Einstein, I think it's safe to assume it's a reliable means by which to deduce other facts about the state of the universe, so here goes.

Science cannot prove that the afterlife does not exist; therefore, just like Schrödinger's cat being both dead and alive, the afterlife must both exist *and* not exist. So thanks to the logic of quantum mechanics in the form of the Schrödinger's cat theory, science has proven the possible existence of the afterlife! Isn't that great?

I'm guessing that you are completely underwhelmed by that conclusion. But this groundwork is important. In later chapters, we'll be going into great detail about what the afterlife is and what you do there, but as the expression goes, we need to walk before we can run. As such, we need a solid foundation to build everything else upon. Each chapter in this book provides another piece of the puzzle which will eventually reveal everything.

So, science has proven the possible existence of the afterlife. You'll notice I said it has proven the *possible* existence. That's because it is impossible to outright prove it with our current level of knowledge and technology. Unless you get all woo-woo, which we're not interested in doing because we want an adult discussion here. So we aren't looking to prove it but to amass evidence using as much logic and as many facts as we can lay our hands on.

Now that we've established such an important aspect of our exploration of the afterlife, we can build upon that and then dig deep into the really good stuff — the nitty-gritty of actually "living" your afterlife, i.e., what you actually do there, where you do it, and how you do it.

However, let me address two crucial points before we press on.

Firstly, is the afterlife dependent on religion?

Some scholars believe that religion — each and every one — came about purely so that people could feel warm and fuzzy about death, believing that when it came, they wouldn't simply fail to exist but move on to something bigger and better. Thousands of years later, many of the less ardent religious followers among us still pretty much find solace in religion for that very same reason. So how does religion impact our exploration of the afterlife?

The answer depends on whether or not you believe in God and, if you do, how strong your faith is. A strong believer will say, yes, the afterlife is dependent on God. Which is fine for the believers, but what about the nonbelievers? Does this mean everyone else is destined to either vanish the instant they die, spend eternity in some kind of limbo, or even go straight to hell?

For a number of reasons, that's simply not logical and not in alignment with most religious teachings. At the risk of upsetting the most religious of readers, it wouldn't put God in a very nice light. Would God, the supreme being of goodness, punish someone for all eternity purely because they made the simple mistake of believing He wasn't real? That's egotistical and God does not suffer flaws such as ego, making it self-contradictory. Further, if that were to be the case, what's happened to forgiveness? Isn't that one of the core pillars of most religions, especially Christianity?

Strangely, while many atheists don't believe in the afterlife, a surprising number do, though obviously without any sort of deity at its heart. For nonbelievers, saying the afterlife is dependent upon the existence of God is like saying the Earth is dependent upon the existence of God, which to them is wrong. The afterlife is, in its simplest terms, merely another "place." Why couldn't another "place" have come into existence in just the same way that the earth did? Of course it could. As astronomy is now proving with the number of Earthlike worlds it is identifying, the Earth is not unique. In fact, the most recent estimates suggest there are, literally, billions of planets similar to ours (billions, yes, that's not a typo — the universe really is so big). So, if the Earth isn't unique and simply came into being, why couldn't this other "place" do likewise?

Secondly, you might believe in the afterlife already, in which case you might want to dispense with any preamble to get straight into the "good stuff" that I've promised. You might be thinking that what I've said so far could be perceived as merely playing with words when what you are desperately craving is "real" answers. Don't worry, those start coming on the very next page.

We've already acknowledged that faith alone is not enough to provide solid answers, so if we want to uncover the truth, we must dig deep. To do that, we must embrace anything and everything that helps us because this subject is so incredibly difficult to pin down. By using this approach, piece by piece, we'll unveil the puzzle that is the afterlife and see it — for the very first time — in glorious Technicolor.

Let me show you what I mean...

What is the Soul?

Before we discuss the nature of the soul, there's an important question we need to answer.

Why do we cling to the notion of a soul?

The soul, the spirit, a person's essence... call it what you will, it's been a constant source of both joy and frustration for centuries because no one has ever been able to prove whether or not it's real.

For many of us, the root of the problem is threefold:

Problem 1

We have big egos — truly massive — so most of us can't imagine that when we die, we simply stop existing. The existence of a soul would mean we continue on, for eternity, which gives us comfort.

Problem 2

We can't bear to think of never seeing loved ones again after they've died. The existence of a soul gives us a lifeline, hope that one day we'll be reunited, so what better concept could we believe in?

Problem 3

We struggle to imagine that all we are is a lump of meat and bones and that the cherished thing we call "I" is nothing but a collection of chemical processes. We ache to believe we are *more*. That the thing that makes each of us unique isn't just biological but deeper, special. So special that we are indefinable. For once a thing is definable, boring scientists can analyze it in boring microscopic detail in boring black and white in boring textbooks. Once so defined, we are forever boring black and white too, when in reality, we are color, we are vibrant, we are effervescent.

When we think like this, it's not surprising that we are drawn to the idea of an "essence" that is so unique to each of us that it transcends this earthly life.

However, there's a heck of a lot of us "believing" and "imagining" going on in those three reasons for believing in the soul, isn't there? That doesn't bode well for the soul existing. If this were a court of law, the prosecution would jump all over that and would leave the judge with no option but to dismiss the "evidence" as insubstantial, or hearsay, or even perjury. The only obvious verdict from such unreliable and damning testimony is that the soul does not exist. Case dismissed.

Sorry to disappoint you, but that's sometimes how the cookie—

Hold your horses, I'm messing with you.

Now, we could easily use the Schrödinger's cat principle again to prove the soul exists. However, we can't dump everything on that poor imprisoned pussycat, so let's see what else we can do.

Fortunately, the lawyer for the defense has a few cards up his sleeve. When the prosecution calls its witnesses — all experts in the fields of physics, biology, philosophy, etc. — the defense turns the tables.

All those experts testifying that the soul does not exist, guess what they're using — that's right, a heck of a lot of "believing" and "imagining," just the same as the witnesses for the defense. So, if the judge dismissed the defense's arguments on the grounds of hearsay or whatever, then he must also dismiss the prosecution's arguments for exactly the same reason. Especially when it comes to one very important legal standard.

Beyond a reasonable doubt.

If you've read a lot of novels set in court, studied the law, or watched TV shows featuring trials, you've no doubt heard that phrase on numerous occasions. If you haven't done any of those things, you may have come across it in news articles. If you haven't, essentially, it means that if someone is being tried in a criminal case, the jury can only convict if they are persuaded — beyond a reasonable doubt — that the defendant is guilty. In other words, for the defendant to be found guilty, the lawyers for the prosecution must prove that there is no other reasonable explanation for how the crime was committed or who committed it. It's called the burden of proof and in the majority of cases, ensures people get a fair trial.

What's this got to do with what we're interested in?

That principle of burden of proof is very interesting. You see, it wasn't just adopted arbitrarily but developed over decades to be one of the cornerstones of the modern justice system because it is based on fairness and, crucially, logic. (Though of course, this system isn't perfect, but that's a topic for another book.)

This means that as a reasoned argument cannot prove beyond a reasonable doubt that the soul does not exist, the only logical conclusion any reasonable person can draw is that the soul *could* exist. (Likewise, the preponderance of the evidence standard of civil law would make it even easier to draw such a conclusion because the burden of proof is replaced by a requirement to show that the evidence is merely enough to tip the scales one way or the other.)

Establishing that the soul *could* exist is not the kind of definitive answer we'd like, but such a position is simply impossible to reach for all the reasons previously mentioned; however, it is reassuring that logic continues to help us in our quest for answers.

So, let's find more of those.

Remember the short quiz you took where I asked questions including what form you'd take in the afterlife? That was essentially asking what you believe your soul will be like after you die.

You'll be surprised to learn this, but every answer could be considered as correct in its own way, except the one about becoming an angel. Angels are a unique creation of God, not something that humans evolve into. Sorry to disappoint you if you had your heart set on that. However, it's not all bad news because the afterlife is going to be so incredible for you that you won't miss that one small wish going unfulfilled.

Space and time will work differently in the afterlife, so your form will be different from what you probably imagine too. It will be able to adopt both incorporeal and corporeal-like forms, i.e., take on a physical-like form or an energy-like form. You'll note I said "energy-like." This is because we most often think of energy in this context as electricity, or something akin to it. This idea is bolstered by some of our everyday expressions — for example, the life "force," or the "spark" of life.

Our own biology would appear to validate this idea too. Biologically, electricity is fundamental to our bodies functioning properly, with everything from our thoughts to nerve impulses using it. The jump to imagine our soul is something like electricity, therefore, is quite small and easy to make. Especially as electricity can pass through some things, has no perceivable weight, and suggests a being of an ethereal quality. It makes it sound ideal, doesn't it?

However, I'd prefer to compare the soul to something other than straightforward electricity for a number of reasons, the main three being:

1. Electricity cannot pass through everything, meaning it has strict limitations.

2. Electricity shocks living things, causing burns and possibly even fatalities.

3. It's most often generated by or housed in a physical body, be that the spinning of Earth's core, the impulses inside the brain, or the weaponry of a stingray.

So what do I prefer as a form of energy?

There are a number of options.

Radiation is one possibility. I know most people will immediately attach bad connotations to that word, thinking of nuclear radiation leaks or nuclear attack and fallout. However, the sunlight is a form of radiation. Conversely to nuclear radiation, visible light, that which illuminates our daily lives and without which life on Earth would be impossible, is a type of radiation that's always viewed positively. So much so that some people imagine becoming beings made of light in the afterlife.

While solid opaque objects block visible light, other forms of radiation can pass through some such things, such as X-rays, microwaves, radio waves, and gamma rays. These are all part of the electromagnetic spectrum. Which leads to another interesting point.

Some researchers believe electromagnetism may have something to do with consciousness, maybe even by creating it. If considered as distinct from the soul, consciousness can, at the very least, be thought of as a close blood relative, making electromagnetic radiation intriguing, should these researchers be correct.

As a slight aside, this illustrates one of the problems we'll be facing on our journey to uncover the wonders of the universe. You see, consciousness is indefinable by science. Scientists cannot say what it is, where it originates, or what it's made up of. All they know is that it cannot be reduced to neural activity — i.e., it is not simply an electrical impulse jumping from one speck of meat to another speck of meat. In other words, there must be more to it.

For example, the actual feeling of happiness can be "viewed" in a scan of the brain by the areas that light up, but this is only a "representation" of the feeling, not the feeling itself. This means what we think, feel, and sense through our consciousness cannot be reduced to mere activity in the brain. There is something else going on, but we simply don't know what. Neuroscience has existed for over one hundred years, and yet it cannot say where consciousness resides or how it does what it does. All neuroscience can tell us is that consciousness is real.

Yet despite this failure to fully understand consciousness, all scientists at least agree on one thing — it exists because, to state the blindingly obvious again, every scientist is conscious and aware. Now, if science can determine little about consciousness except that it exists, we shouldn't be surprised that science has drawn such a blank on the existence of the soul.

Consciousness and the soul, if not one and the same, are so closely linked, they're inseparable. After all, the soul is more closely related to the consciousness than to the body by its very nature, so that's not surprising. As ever, science can't help us with this distinction either. However, many respected scientists believe in mind-body dualism, i.e., that there are two distinct types of "substance" in the universe, one being physical and the other nonphysical. Some have even used our old friend Schrödinger's cat to prove this, believing that only by a conscious being opening the box to look at the cat does the cat become either alive or dead. Until that point — the intrusion of consciousness — the cat is both alive and dead, which is termed a superposition state (the ability for something to be in two or more states at the same time).

Now, let's get back to the form the soul may take.

The other option to explain the form the soul may take is something akin to gravity. While that doesn't have the dazzle that a "light being" may have, gravity has other qualities that make it fascinating. For instance, it affects everything — literally, everything. The gravity of a large mass can be so strong it can even change time and space. Now, that's power. Also, gravity affects everything it touches. Unlike visible light, which is blocked by any opaque object, or X-rays and gamma rays, which can't penetrate lead, there hasn't been a material found yet that can resist gravity's effect.

Gravity, however, is a very different animal from electromagnetic radiation. So much so, it would be impractical to imagine a being "made" of gravity. So why do I mention it? Remember the rhino analogy? The discussion of gravity is to give you a concrete example of the forces that surround us, some of which are so powerful that they are completely unstoppable and can influence everything in their vicinity. This will be an important point as we dig deeper into both the soul and the afterlife.

However, the interest in gravity doesn't stop there, not least for one very big reason.

Some scientists, including some Nobel Prize winners, believe there might be a relationship between quantum mechanics and consciousness. (If you've never heard of quantum mechanics, it's a branch of physics that deals with how matter and light behave on a subatomic and atomic level.) Cutting-edge research is currently being conducted to discover if there is a link between quantum mechanics and consciousness, and if so, how it is possible that the physical world can be influenced by the nonphysical. These researchers believe gravity may be involved in how the physical world and the nonphysical interact. Gravity is full of surprises, isn't it?

So there are two contenders for the form the soul might take, yet there can be only one answer. So, what do we do? The obvious — combine the ideas.

That gives us a being taking an energy-like form that is capable of influencing its environment in a comparable manner to the way in which gravity influences its environment.

But that's hard to picture, isn't it? And I said I was going to make things simple, didn't I?

Remember above, where I said the soul could be both corporeal and incorporeal, having both a physical-like form and an energy-like form? Why did I make that distinction? What is the point and how would that work?

The point is very simple — can a light beam hold your hand?

Of course not. And yet, one of the most appealing factors for most of us in the existence of an afterlife is the possibility of meeting lost loved ones. That's appealing to me, and I'm sure it is to you, yes?

So here's where it gets interesting. Imagine being able to transform from a nonphysical form into a physical-like one. That means you can enjoy that one-on-one connection that makes life so worth living — the touch of another being. (Note that I said "being" there and not "person" — I have animal friends I want to hug again. I bet you do too.)

And while the concept of nonphysical entities being able to touch might sound like magic, as physics tells us, matter can be converted into energy, so why shouldn't an energy being be able to take a material form? Simple, huh? Especially as some scientists argue matter and energy are virtually the same thing.

If only there was some way science could help us out here by giving us an example of something that can actually do that — be both physical and nonphysical.

Hmmm. You're not going to believe this, but...

To survive on earth, at the very least, we need food, water, sleep, shelter, and air. A lack of any one of those things can cause health issues, and the longer the absence persists, the deeper those issues become, possibly even proving fatal.

But what do we need in the afterlife?

We don't have a physical form like the one we have on earth, so we don't have the limitations of such a form and the dependence such forms have on sustenance and protection.

But how?

It's estimated that the sun will live for around eleven billion years. As such, it's the oldest thing any of us will ever have experience of, so to speak, because we feel its effect every single day of our lives. And yet, one day, something so huge and so powerful will burn out. Effectively, die.

So if even the sun will die, how can a soul exist forever?

It's easy if you believe in God, because then you believe some things last forever, but what if you don't believe?

Science states that the universe is around fourteen billion years old. But how do scientists know?

Simple: they measured something called background radiation, which has been around since the universe came into being. This background radiation is a form of electromagnetic radiation — see where I'm going with this?

Yep, we've already discussed electromagnetic radiation.

If background radiation can "survive" for as long as the universe has been in existence, then that's literally forever! Problem solved.

Well...

Sadly, no, that hasn't solved the issue.

The problem is that this background radiation is fading. Eventually, it will become so faint, we will no longer be able to detect it. One day, it too will be gone altogether.

So, even if the soul was energy-like, similar to some form of electromagnetic radiation, could it last literally forever?

The answer comes from a surprising source.

I first heard of a photon on a 1960s TV show that I loved as a kid — *Star Trek*. In the heat of battle, Captain James T. Kirk would instruct Lieutenant Sulu, the helmsman, to fire photon torpedoes. That sounded so cool!

Of course, I had no idea what a photon was, but that didn't stop my excitement from rising the instant that order was given.

So, what is a photon?

A photon can be most easily thought of as a tiny particle *or* tiny wave of light. Simple, huh? Except, like many things we're considering, it is far, far from simple!

You see, when we usually think of a particle, we think of a "lump" of something, which a photon isn't. A photon is massless, i.e., it has no "body," for want of a better analogy, so there is no "lump" that you could weigh.

Also — and get this! — a photon does not experience time.

To a photon, there is no past, present, or future. If a photon hits some form of matter, then it will be absorbed or scattered. However, if it never hits anything, it will "live" forever. It is, in effect, ageless.

So, a photon can be immortal. It doesn't need food, sleep, water, air. It doesn't wear out or become sick.

But if you recall, I just said a photon could be thought of as both a tiny particle and a tiny wave of light. This has been proven by science and yet a particle is physical while a wave is nonphysical. How is that possible?

Science can't tell us. All science can tell us is that this dual state is fact.

So if a photon can be corporeal and incorporeal, both a physical particle and a nonphysical wave, why can't something else be too? Like the soul?

As if that isn't mind-blowing enough, photons don't experience distance the way we do but can instantaneously travel anywhere. Even more amazing is that they can be in two places at once — which will be extremely pertinent later. (Talk about a cliffhanger!)

So, photons give a lot of clues as to what is and what isn't possible for a being made of energy.

And as photons are light, it leads into another way of imagining how a being made of energy, possibly light, could be both physical and nonphysical.

Think hologram technology.

A holographic person is essentially a being made of light, which is what we're talking about. But if that technology were taken to the next level so sophisticated sensors could be introduced to, in effect, give the holographic person means to scan their environment, like a rudimentary nervous system, that person could "feel" the touch of another holographic person. This isn't technology that's likely to be available in the foreseeable future, but we're not discussing engineering — we're trying to wrap our heads around the idea of a light being having the ability to interact in a physical-like way. And this provides it. (Sci-fi fans will grasp this in an instant, with the likes of *Star Trek*, *The Matrix*, and *Red Dwarf* having used such concepts to create holographic and digital characters.)

Now, before you go dismissing this on the grounds that it is pure science fiction, researchers around the world are making technological breakthroughs all the time. For instance, some have discovered a way to create a three-dimensional shape using ultrasound that people can literally touch, even though there's nothing actually there.

To be able to touch something that isn't there sounds crazy, but think of it this way. When you were a kid, did you ever hold two magnets together? If you held them the right way, they stuck together, but if held the opposite way, they repelled each other. I remember being fascinated by that "feeling" of them pushing each other apart — that bouncy, curvy, smooth "feeling" as if a physical thing was between them. Like touching something that wasn't there.

Of course, some people would say this entire conversation is moot anyway, stating there's no need for a physical form because the love between two people would be bond enough.

And of course that is vitally important — love is the only point of experiencing the afterlife.

While most of us experience the love of a parent, a sibling, a friend, a partner, a relative, a child, or a pet, some are lucky enough to experience more than one of those, if not all of them. So we know what love feels like. That warmth when we're with the other person. That sense of security. Of reassurance. Of being wanted, respected, and appreciated. Of belonging. We feel it, often, and yet we still seek physical contact — whether that be a handshake, a hug, or sexual intimacy. It's as if we are programmed to need physical contact, to literally need the touch of another being to live a fulfilling life. So that is why it is important that the soul can take two distinct forms, or at least interact as if it can.

Here, I'm not necessarily talking about a soul that is composed of energy one second, then transforms into a humanlike being the next. Though the form may take the appearance of a human and have some of the qualities associated with it — for instance, the ability to feel, taste, see, etc. — this is a different realm, where different rules apply, so this form, while it may look human, is not human, but something better.

Better?

How?

That's what we're about to get into right after we find out...

What — and When — is the Afterlife?

In July 2022, I visited Warsaw, Poland, with my Polish partner, Kasia. One lazy afternoon, we ambled around the suburb of Mokotow, where an area around one hundred yards by five hundred yards is divided into small plots on which people tend gardens and relax in single-story wooden summer houses. Most gardens bloomed with flowers, but I was stunned at the number containing trees heavy with fruit — apples, pears, plums, cherries...

Gazing wistfully at an apple tree, Kasia said, "It reminds me of Gidle."

Over the years, she's told me countless tales about long, lazy childhood summers in her great-grandparents' tiny village.

"Yes?" I picked up a snail from the middle of the concrete path and placed it on the grass, where it would be safe.

Kasia said, "One time, my great-grandma scolded me because I ate so many gooseberries straight off the bush that there weren't enough left for her pie."

I laughed, picturing her gorging on berries till her belly swelled.

But instead of laughing too, she wiped away a tear.

I touched her arm. "What's wrong?"

"I'll never see that place again." Her chin trembled. "Everyone's dead, and the house has been torn down and the garden dug up to be redeveloped."

Her face twisted with the pain of loss.

I hugged her. "I'm sorry."

"When I die, if there's a heaven, that's where I want to be."

"In Gidle?"

She nodded. "A little girl on holiday at my great-grandparents' house. Forever."

"So how about me? If you're six years old, where do I fit in?"

"I'm sorry, David, but that time in Gidle is so special. That's where I want to be. Even if it means losing everything else."

I squeezed her hand and smiled at her. "What if you don't have to?"

She squinted at me. "Don't have to what?"

"Don't have to lose anything."

"How?"

I shared part of what I'm about to share with you.

Kasia cried again. Except this time, they weren't tears of sadness but tears of joy.

It was this innocent conversation that led to this book. It might sound like these insights came in an instant, like divine inspiration. No. They've been percolating in my mind for decades; I just never sat down to give them the attention they needed for everything to fit together like a jigsaw puzzle.

Now, as we get into the really juicy stuff, some of the things we'll be discussing might at first seem a little "out there." You might figure they are simply too crazy to believe. And to be honest, I don't blame you because, yes, some of these concepts are revolutionary. But let me ask you a question.

What would you say if I told you that I know of a place where gold literally falls from out of the sky?

You'd think I was either lying or crazy, wouldn't you?

And that's understandable. Especially because I am lying in saying that.

But ask me if I know of a place where lead literally falls from out of the sky.

Go on. Ask. I dare you.

You know where this is going now, don't you? Even though it sounds utterly preposterous that lead could ever drop out of the sky, now you've got a tiny inkling that maybe I know something that you don't.

And you'd be right!

But before I come clean, here's another question for you — what is snow made of?

If you said frozen water... well, you're kind of right. But also kind of wrong. You see, it depends on where that snow is falling.

Here, snow is made up of frozen water, yes. However, on the planet Venus, it snows lead. Literally. Tiny specks of lead drop out of the sky.

It's almost impossible to imagine a place where the snow is tiny chunks of metal, isn't it? And yet it's true. (It's actually a substance called Lead(II) sulfide.)

So, the moral here is that we must keep an open mind. It's unbelievably easy for us to make rash judgments about something, when in truth, we possess zero knowledge of it to actually have a reasoned opinion either way. I can't tell you the times that jumping to the wrong conclusion because I didn't have all the facts has landed me in hot water! I'm sure you know just what I mean.

But back to Kasia.

She obviously had an image of the afterlife in her mind. A paradise built around her most cherished childhood memories. But is she right to imagine the afterlife could be like this?

Heaven.

What images does that conjure for you?

Picture it. Go on. Close your eyes for a few seconds and picture an image of what you want it to be.

What did you see?

Let me take a stab at your vision...

A paradise: this is a magnificent landscape like something conjured in a computer for a Hollywood blockbuster movie. Wondrous waterfalls tumble over cliffs, lush greenery like spring comes every day and gushes everywhere, exotic creatures wander around, calm, unafraid, and friendly. Here, you walk through breathtaking scenery with your loved ones, marveling at the spectacle while basking in togetherness.

A traditional image: an astral realm filled with harps, angels, and ancient architecture of sculpted stone columns and arches. Here, you spend your days praising the Lord, meeting loved ones, or expanding your mind. In between which you can watch over family members who are still on earth.

Bliss: here, heaven isn't a "place" but a cosmic pool of love that, like the ocean, buoys you, so you endlessly drift beside the love of your life, warmed by their closeness.

Home is where the heart is: heaven is a replica of your home, or something similar with the same loving feel, only bigger and grander. You spend your days surrounded by grandparents, parents, siblings, children, friends... everyone you've ever loved who has passed on. This new home is an oasis of caring, sharing, and love.

Or maybe you picture something entirely different from any of those.

Whatever you envision, I'm sure it was beautiful, but here's the thing — fasten your seat belt because you're not going to like it!

What you imagined is impossible and could never work.

See, I told you that you wouldn't like it. But don't panic!

Before you get upset, let me explain the simple mistake you've made and how the reality of what you'll find in the afterlife will be even better than your wildest imaginings.

If you recall, Kasia wanted to spend her afterlife as a six-year-old girl staying with her great-grandparents in the country.

That sounds reasonable, doesn't it? Not to mention doable. At first glance, yes, but unfortunately, under scrutiny it breaks down into an unworkable mess because you run slap-bang into all kinds of problems, contradictions, and impossibilities.

You see, her great-grandmother and great-grandfather are in heaven with her, so what about what they want their afterlife to consist of? What if their idea of heaven is for them not to be old and frail but to be young lovers, eternally reveling in the joy of their first month together in the city, not their final years in the country. That's completely different from Kasia's afterlife. It means Kasia's heaven is entirely dependent on all her loved ones dreaming of a heaven that fits only her dream and not their own dream. That makes Kasia's scenario heaven for her, but definitely not for anyone else.

And this is just one of the reasons why the traditional view of heaven is unworkable.

But don't despair, because a version of that heaven is very achievable with just a simple shift in mindset. You see, to "live" in the afterlife means we have to be supremely adaptable. On first reading, what I'm about to suggest may seem odd, in fact, very odd, but I guarantee the more you think about it, the more you'll appreciate the beauty in it and how it is the *only* way the afterlife can work.

So, what's the mind shift we have to talk about?

Hold on to your hat because this is where things get exciting!

The afterlife is not located in one specific place, but instead, it consists of an infinite number of places, all of which are created by you, and me, and everyone else there. In other words, it is dimensionless. Outside space. An alternate world. Whatever you want to call it along those lines, that's what it is.

Let me explain.

In order for you to interact with your loved ones, or any being, there must be a "place," but just because there is a "place" where you interact doesn't mean that is the same place where every other person in the afterlife resides.

That probably sounds like gobbledygook, yes?

Here's the thing — the afterlife doesn't abide by the same laws of time and space as we do here on earth.

Take a moment to let that settle in.

That's a huge concept, so let me break it down for you so you can see what I mean and how it's not only the only logical solution but the best solution *for us*.

I'll illustrate the situation with an example.

Say you live a happy family-oriented life, being close to your maternal grandparents, your mother, partner, and son. Once you and they have all passed over, obviously your main wish will be to spend time with all of them.

But "which" them?

Remember the quiz you took — what age did you say you were in the afterlife?

The majority of people imagine being fit, healthy, and youthful, so for illustrative purposes, we'll say everyone is around twenty-five years old. That's great on one level, but how does that work if your beloved childhood memories include climbing onto your grandpa's knee on an evening to snuggle up and watch TV? You're twenty-five *and* he's twenty-five. Sitting in his lap is just plain weird. It means that treasured memory is truly dead because it can't possibly work. So while this option of being a certain age has some benefits, it also has major drawbacks.

As for one of the other options to forever be the age you were when you died, that's probably the most depressing idea ever. What if you died at ninety? Do you want to spend eternity stooped, frail, saggy, gray...? (Incontinent – we won't even go there!)

But it gets worse.

What if you died as you were born? That means eternity as a baby less than a day old. Is that how you always pictured heaven working? Not me!

Okay, so maybe in the afterlife you believe you can choose the age you'll be. Great. What could go wrong there?

Back to our example family – you live such a long and, overall, wonderful life, but most of it was alone after your first relationship fell apart. The only good thing coming out of that was your daughter. However, fate has a wonderful gift – in your fifties, you meet a new partner and your life gets better and better. Eventually, you die, so being free to choose your afterlife age, in this scenario, you opt for fifty-three, the best year of your life.

But your partner, who you want to spend eternity with, also gets to choose for themselves, and they choose twenty-two.

Okay, that's not a huge problem because there aren't the taboos in the afterlife that there are on earth, so fifty-three and twenty-two isn't an issue.

But your mother wants to be twenty-six. That's the age she was when she had you, when her life with your father had seemed perfect.

Your mom being twenty-seven years younger than you will be odd, to say the least.

However, there's also your grandparents. They both died while you were still a child, so you cherish the few memories you have of them. Unfortunately, your grandparents both want to be sixteen, longing to relive their years as childhood sweethearts. But where does that leave you wanting to relive sitting on Grandpa's knee — a fifty-three-year-old sitting in the lap of a sixteen-year-old? Even when we're talking about heaven, a place filled with love, forgiveness, and tolerance, that feels a little off, doesn't it? That aside, it makes it impossible for you to reestablish that loving connection with your grandparents because they are now not just young but people you never knew. Even if everyone retains all their memories no matter what age they choose to appear, it's still a weird scenario to have parents and grandparents who are younger than you are. It alters the dynamic between you, and suddenly, *your* heaven has a weird undercurrent that makes you struggle with relationships — which is the last thing you want in the afterlife, isn't it?

And just when you think things can't get any worse...

Your son, being the youngest of all of you, is the last to arrive in the afterlife. He's lived a remarkable life, so remarkable that he chooses to honor it by remaining the age he was when he died — ninety-two.

You are thirty-nine years younger than your son. Nearly two generations apart in the wrong direction.

It must be clear from all this that choosing your own age is fraught with difficulties.

So where does that leave us?

We started off this chapter discussing where the afterlife was, but we seem to have veered into something completely different. Except, we haven't. Trust me, because as we explore further, we'll circle right back and everything will click into place and we'll have the afterlife running like a fine Swiss watch. Which isn't only an apt simile...

Time. That's the key.

How can you recapture that love and happiness you had with loved ones when some of them are a world away from the memories you cherish?

It's down to the way time works and how we use it. And I mean use it in a literal sense, like we'd use a tool.

You see, time doesn't work the way we understand it does on earth. In fact, time doesn't work the way we believe it does. Period.

So how does time work in heaven? I'm sure you're a little wary of "messing" with time because as humans, we only ever experience time flowing in an unending straight line going from our birth to our death, but never going in the opposite direction (unless it's in Hollywood movies like *Back To The Future*). During life, for us, time is one of the most reliable constants we have. Except it isn't. In reality, time is far from constant, so prepare to rethink everything you believe you know about it.

If you believe in God, this will be easy to grasp with a simple example (if you don't believe, don't worry because we'll come to that in a moment, but continue reading so you get a clear picture of the full scenario).

Okay, so the traditional view of the Christian God is that He is all-powerful and all-knowing, so He sees the past, present, and future simultaneously. For Him, yesterday, today, and tomorrow are all happening before His eyes, whereas for us living on earth, the past has gone and can't be reached again, the future hasn't yet arrived, so it could go off in any number of directions, and the present is so fleeting, we can't even contemplate it before the moment becomes the past. Tricky, huh?

Before we move ahead, I think it wise to look more closely at one of those points in particular. Let's look at what we think of as the "present" and how we handle it.

We handle the present in one simple way — we make constant predictions about what is going to happen, second by second, hour by hour, day by day. Much of them subconscious. If we didn't make these constant predictions, we'd live in a perpetual state of anxiety and chaos.

What do I mean by "predictions"? We "predict" that the brakes will work on our car when we need them. We "predict" our stove will heat our food when we turn it on. We "predict" an elevator will go up when we press the button to do so. We believe in such predictions because experience has told us that the favored outcome is what will happen, except it doesn't always. If instead we focused on the brakes not working, the stove burning our house down, or the elevator plummeting us to our deaths, which, though unlikely, are very real possibilities, everyday life would be unmanageable. So, it's our judicious use of predictions, based on our beliefs of likely outcomes, that allows us to function.

Further, to get really granular about how we think of time, especially the present, consider the following concept: for just a few seconds, stop reading, look around you, and notice what is happening, then come back.

So what happened?

Maybe you're at home and someone is clicking through the channels on the TV.

Or maybe you're in a park and kids are kicking a ball around.

You might think that is what is happening *in the present*. And why wouldn't you? You literally just witnessed it with your own eyes.

But you didn't.

Even though what you saw appeared to be happening *right now*, what you witnessed happening was actually in the past. Light travels at 186,000 miles per second. That's so fast it's impossible to imagine. And yet, even that speed means it takes light a certain time to travel a certain distance. This means that every single thing you see in the world around you has happened in the past because it has taken the light a certain length of time to reach you, not to mention the extra time for your brain to process what it is seeing. What you see immediately around you might only have happened a microsecond ago, but it is still the past. And this relates to every single thing. But more, the farther away a thing is, the "older" is the view of it that you see because it takes light that fraction longer to reach you. That means that when you look at someone sitting beside you on the sofa, they are actually closer to your "present" than someone sitting at the far side of the room. Freaky or what?

I know this is difficult to get your head around, so I'll give you a concrete example. You must have witnessed a thunderstorm. Must have seen lightning and then, moments later, heard the rumble of thunder. The lightning and the thunder happened at exactly the same time and yet, because of how far you were from them and the vast difference in the speed of light and the speed of sound, you saw the flash of lightning and then afterward heard the crash of thunder. That thunder was you witnessing the past as if it was your present. And the further away you are from the lightning, the longer it will take the sound of the thunder to reach you, so the further into the past it happened.

Externally to us, there is no such thing as the present. Internally, by the time we've thought about "this" moment as being the present, the moment is past.

Get ready for something weird!

And I mean *weird*. Maybe the weirdest thing you'll ever read.

Look at your hand.

Ready for a shocking revelation?

That isn't your hand. That *was* your hand. Even though it's part of your own body, you are still seeing it "in the past." Your hand is simply another object from which it takes time for light to travel. Plus, it takes extra time for your mind to process what you are seeing. This is how you burn yourself by touching something hot — your nervous system and mind need a fraction of a second to register the heat, by which time it's already too late and the heat has done its damage. Every part of your body is already in the past. Freaky or what?

We never — *never* — experience the world as it is *right now!* We only ever experience the past.

But it gets freakier because we don't experience just the past but different "pasts." Because everything is at varying distances from us, everything we see exists in a different time in the past. This amount of time might only be counted in nanoseconds, with one nanosecond being one-billionth of a second, but even so, that is a *real* time difference.

Don't be fooled into thinking that because a nanosecond is so incredibly tiny, it doesn't matter. One nanosecond might seem tiny, but the implications of this concept are gigantic.

Further, it's only tiny because of our preconceived notion of time. The sun is over four billion years old and will last for around another seven billion years. That's eleven billion years. To the sun, eighty years is meaningless, yet for most of us, that's an entire lifetime. Time is relative. It cannot be dismissed on the basis of the amount of it being discussed.

The duration of one nanosecond is tiny, yes, but that does not make it meaningless. A single cent is tiny compared to a thousand dollars but it is still real money.

So, even though a nanosecond is such a tiny amount of time, what we experience in our perceived present can be way, way back in the past. So far back, it can be counted in years.

For example, when we sit outside with our partner and marvel at the stars, we see and hear what our partner does and says only a tiny fraction of a second in the past, but the starlight bathing us has taken so long to reach us that what we are actually seeing is so old that the dinosaurs were still alive on earth when that light first shone. And every single thing in the space between our partner and the stars is in a different past time because it's at a different distance from us.

In other words, if your partner stands before you, with the stars behind them, you are seeing both what happened a tiny fraction of a second ago (your partner) and what happened tens of millions years ago (when the starlight was born and the world was filled with tyrannosaurs, stegosaurs, pterosaurs...).

Even the light from our sun takes over eight minutes to reach us. Eight minutes. That means it could literally blow up and for eight whole minutes, we wouldn't know and would simply carry on as normal.

We all take time for granted, take it as an absolute, and yet it is so incredibly complex, it's verging on the unperceivable to both our senses and our intellect. Luckily, we've found ways around this.

To compensate for every moment of the present disappearing into the past, we usually think of the present in terms of the next day or two, or even a few weeks, but what we are truly thinking in doing this is not the "present" but the "near future." This near future is easier to predict but can blow up in our faces at any moment — if you've ever jumped at a sound, let something slip from your grasp, or been in a car crash, it illustrates how your perception of the how the "present" was unfolding was actually a prediction of the future which you got wrong and the real event surprised you. This "near future" is usually very predictable, but it can't be relied upon to be so, which can deliver anything from a pleasant surprise to a tragic event.

What does all this mean in the grand scheme of things?

That we live in a delusion — the present, as we think of it, does not exist. Time is not what we believe it to be. So let's see what it is because how it truly works changes everything for us.

God doesn't have the problems with the past and future that we have — we aren't able to return to the past, while the future is anything from safe and steady to unpredictable chaos. He sees everything as if it were all happening right now, right in front of Him. (We'll get to how this works for nonbelievers soon.)

Now, if you accept the existence of God, you must accept that He can see past, present, and future. Therefore, you have already accepted that while time works in a linear fashion for us on earth, it works differently for God. You have also, therefore, accepted that time is not an absolute, not a constant that can never vary in speed or in direction. Your acceptance of God means you accept these ideas, whether you've ever thought about it before or not.

Here's the fun thing — if God can do that with time, then why shouldn't another being be able to view time differently? I'm not asking why another being can't be all-powerful, and thereby be God, but if we've proven that time is malleable for one being, then logically, there is no reason why it couldn't be malleable for another, though at a vastly reduced scale so that being wasn't gifted with godlike powers.

Now, if you're religious, you may balk at that because it may seem to go against God by diminishing His power. But it actually does the complete opposite. Here's how.

Time being malleable for other beings, i.e., us, is borne out by the fact that God grants us eternal life in His kingdom. Eternal life means time must no longer function as it does for us on earth. For example, I'm guessing that God doesn't allow us to age as we do on earth — eternal life wouldn't be much fun if you were 2,384 years old and felt it! So in this scenario, time is *not* time as we know it.

Further, for you not to age, God cannot constantly rejuvenate your body, because doing so acknowledges that you have aged and that God is reversing the effect, so the only option is for God to stop your cells from aging in the first place.

God has, in effect, stopped time for your cells, and thereby for you. This is another example of how time in the afterlife cannot be thought of in the same way as it can on earth. (The same can be said for an energy-like form — energy drains, even our sun will die at some point, so because energy isn't everlasting, but we are supposed to be, God must stop time.)

Here's an alternative way to look at it, which you might prefer.

God sees past, present, and future all at once. That's accepted. Plus, He's also supposed to be, literally, everywhere. Again, that's accepted.

With both of those accepted, it isn't much of a stretch to believe that a person's soul can mimic those abilities to a much lesser degree. Why? Because God made us in His image, didn't He? That means that the existence of God suggests it is possible for you to be in two different places at the same time, and that time in those two places does not have to run in sync the way we are used to it doing.

So, in a Christian afterlife, time must work differently. *Must.* That's a given. It must, or eternal life would very, very rapidly become eternal hell!

But if time is different from how we've always perceived it to be, how does it work?

God can see all of time. Not least because "all of time" is what concerns Him, because... well, He's God. But us? Really, the main thing that concerns us is our lifetime and that of any progeny. It would seem reasonable, therefore, that God would allow us at the very least to see our entire lifetime, from the moment of our birth to the moment of our death. Anything other than this would just be a rehash of the old linear time we experienced on earth, where time "happens" in a succession of incidents that only move forward, which we've already decided is not what happens in the afterlife.

However, as time is different in the afterlife, not least because, for want of a better expression, we live for eternity, then it means not only should we be able to look back on our lifetime, but we should be able to look back on the whole of history and look forward on the whole of the future.

If that seems problematic, science can help us here with relation to God, which is surprising because science and religion are often mutually exclusive.

While this will sound odd, some physicists believe that time is an illusion. They believe that apart from for our own benefit, time has no purpose and fundamentally doesn't even exist. They propose that we created time as nothing more than a tool to help us live our lives, and that's all it is and all it ever will be. Period.

The important element for us in this is that if time doesn't exist, it would explain how God and the soul can exist "forever." You see, in such a scenario, there is no such thing as "forever," because forever is a period of time, and time doesn't exist, so there can be no such period; everything simply "is."

This would also explain how we would be able to view the whole of history — forward and backward — because we would not be looking at past, present, and future but looking at what simply "is."

If you are struggling to imagine such a concept, picture the whole of history as a movie that you've streamed. As such, you can click to see any moment in time that you wish because you are no longer a tiny speck on history's immense timeline, but instead, you are outside of it as an observer.

But we'll leave that particular concept there because it has served its purpose, so we don't need to delve into it any deeper.

Now, buckle up, because we're getting to another juicy part.

So as you can see, you get to view your past life. And not just to view it as if you're watching a movie, but to recreate it and interact with it. Through this recreation, you can, in effect, revisit places and people, and relive events. You can't change the actual events that happened on earth, but there is nothing to stop you from creating new events based on actual ones.

This might sound weird, so we'll explore an example. Say you want to revisit your sixth birthday, when you got your first bike. You want to feel the excitement of your dad taking you out to the garage and of the gleaming red bike waiting for you there. This was such a special moment you shared that you want to relive the anxiety of climbing onto the bike for the first time, to feel the reassuring hand of your dad steadying it for you, and finally, to bask in the thrill of pedaling along the sidewalk for the very first time.

Why shouldn't you experience all of that? Truly experience it, with all the emotion and everything, as opposed to just viewing it as if it were a movie? You can't travel back in time and change the color of the bike, or that your mom held you steady, not your dad, because those events were what actually happened. So you can't change the past. But...

And here's what it gets super cool.

If your parents have died too, there is no reason why they can't revisit that moment with you and expand it to create fresh events to cherish. That thirty minutes of excitement of the original event that you wanted to recapture could easily grow into hours, days, or even weeks of you and your parents "living" a life that didn't happen on earth. This isn't changing the past but merely expanding a recreation of it in one of your created worlds (which will be explained soon). I repeat, you are not changing the past here. You haven't gone back in time. The moment has been recreated for you to relive, so if you choose to develop something else from this particular event, you aren't changing the past but creating something new.

This is fiddly to get your head around, so let's explore it from another angle to make it clearer. Imagine the actual event of you riding your bike for the first time with your dad's help lasted thirty minutes. After that, you dashed back inside and spent ten minutes excitedly telling your mom every tiny detail of your adventure. That entire bike memory covered forty minutes of your life. That is history. That's what actually happened.

However, in your heavenly recreation of the event, you and your dad spend far longer riding up and down the street. Further, your mom comes out, sits on the wall, and applauds and shouts encouragement each time you pass. Your bike riding no longer lasts thirty minutes but now covers an hour.

Here, you are adding to the recreation, not changing the original. And because this extension only happens in the afterlife, where we've established the rules of time are different, it doesn't affect the linear timeline of your life on earth — i.e., your life on earth remains completely unchanged, so human history doesn't change, even on the microscale of your lifetime.

You see, in the afterlife, there is nothing to stop you from branching away from something you revisit to create fresh events, in this instance with you as a child sharing some special time with your parents. This could last anything from a few minutes to a few decades — it's the afterlife, so it's entirely your choice, though there is no actual time period because, as we've established, time works differently, so any period is merely an impression of time created to give an incident realism for your benefit.

But it doesn't stop there.

Say after you've ridden your bike, you and your parents stroll to a nearby park and enjoy ice cream on a bench. This little trip takes another fifty-five minutes. Earthly history shows the actual events in your lifetime took forty minutes, but this afterlife version is 115 minutes. Yet the past has not been changed and your memories of the past have not been changed. That forty-minute section of your life on earth has not changed by one second. The only thing that you've done is recreate a cherished memory and then prolong it by remaining in the same place with the same characters in a world that you created in heaven (this act of "creation" will be explored later). If this is proving a little complex to wrap your head around, don't worry, because as more and more is revealed, everything will get clearer and clearer.

Okay, that's how time works differently from the perspective of those who believe in God, but how does it work if we take Him out of the equation?

Firstly, one of the points above bears up here too — living forever means we don't age. If our cells have been stopped from aging, that has, in effect, stopped time for our cells, and thereby for us. This is a simple example of how time in the afterlife cannot be thought of in the same way as it can on earth.

But there's more.

If you're struggling with the thought that time might not act like the time we understand, here's something to consider.

Time only acts like "time" when we let it! This is going to surprise you, but things like gravity affect time. On a number of occasions, scientists have set two atomic clocks to exactly the same time. The first has remained on the ground while the second was flown at altitude aboard a plane. When the plane landed, the times of the two clocks were compared.

They were different. Seriously, I'm not messing with you.

The one that flew on the plane was ahead of the one that had stayed on the ground. You see, gravity gets weaker the further away from the earth's core you are, so time in the plane moved faster relative to time on the ground. This is called time dilation. But don't worry about remembering this scientific principle; all you need to appreciate is that, unlike what you've been led to believe, time is not an absolute — the fundamental way it works can change depending on the situation.

This experiment has been repeated numerous times over the decades and the result is always the same — the two clocks match at take-off, but on landing, they are out of sync. Every time. Scientists have tested and tested this and are convinced enough by the results to state that gravity affects how time passes. They've also concluded this through studying black holes and the effects caused by the immense gravity these phenomena produce. Time is not the constant most of us have always believed it to be — science has proved it repeatedly.

I hope you can now see that one hour is not always one hour, a day not always a day. And that's only here on earth. The afterlife takes this to the next level and then some. We'll explore more on this and then I'll introduce you to the octopus that is going to make some unbelievably complex concepts unbelievably simple.

Yep, an octopus no less!

Meeting Departed Loved Ones

I don't know about you, but one of the big draws about the afterlife for me is meeting my loved ones again. And not just loved ones in the traditional sense, but in the sense that it matters to me — I count the animals I've shared my life with as family, so meeting them again is vital.

Whether it's a beloved partner, dog, cat, mother, father, sister, brother, friend, or relative, I'm sure you dream of a reunion one day.

But how would such a thing be possible?

We've already discussed the numerous ways the afterlife might function and none of them appear compatible with meeting our loved ones. Mainly because our concept of time doesn't play ball.

And this is where many of the pieces we've discussed slot together.

We've already established that time doesn't abide by the rules as we currently understand them. This is crucial.

Remember my conversation with my Kasia in Poland that started all this? How she longed to be a little girl forever enjoying summer at her great-grandparents' house in the country?

If she did that, and time behaved in the linear fashion we've always accepted it does, then she could never see me again.

I'm going to draw on physics to show you how Kasia can have her cake and eat it. Which means you can too!

Don't panic, but this is a field of physics that is notoriously difficult to grasp. In fact, it's so new and so complex that the scientists exploring it freely admit that they don't understand it themselves. One Nobel laureate reportedly said, "If you think you understand quantum mechanics, you don't understand quantum mechanics."

Luckily, we don't have to understand but only to appreciate that the discoveries they are making in this field have an impact on how we view the whole universe and beyond.

There's a thing called "quantum superposition." Cool name, but the only thing about it that you need to remember is that it shows that one thing can be in two places at the same time. So, not just a cool name, but cool, period. For us, how this is achieved isn't important. The only thing that is important is that this is possible. We know it is because science tells us so! Numerous scientists have proved this by conducting experiments with light.

Now, have you grasped the implications so you're jumping ahead or are you still mulling over such an earth-shattering concept?

And it is earth-shattering.

You see, it proves that one thing can be in two places simultaneously, and if light can do that, why can't something else? You or me, for example? After all, if light can be in two places at once and you are a being made of light...

Unfortunately, it's unbelievably difficult to grasp how that is possible because it simply doesn't make sense to us, it being so far outside of our experience. However, we don't have to worry about "how" it is possible because science has already proven it is. Multiple times. The concept is now accepted as fact by the scientific community, so we can just go with it.

A bigger problem is the concept of another "you," which throws up so many questions.

> Which one of the two "yous" is the real "you"?

> If you are in two places at the same time, how on earth will you follow what the other "you" is doing?

> How do you control or communicate with the other "you"?

No matter which way you look at it, it seems crazy. Utterly impossible.

But is it impossible? Or, similar to the issue we had with time, is it simply the way we are looking at the concept that makes it problematic?

Tell me, can you drive a car while chatting to a friend?

Can you watch TV and scroll through social media?

Can you cook a meal while answering your child's homework questions?

That's multitasking. We all do it to some degree. Right this moment, I'm listening to music as I type. Multitasking. It's the ability to teach ourselves to be able to do one thing with one part of our body while another part does something different. And the more we practice, the easier it all becomes until we can perform such tasks almost on autopilot.

Everyday forms of multitasking are pretty simple, but others are remarkably complex. For example, you must have seen rock stars sing while playing guitar. That's two complex skills being performed at the same time. Impressive, huh? But that's nothing compared to some Air Force pilots who must fly their craft, monitor their airspace, report on the radio, evade enemies, and fire weapons, all while traveling at hundreds of miles per hour. Which sounds hard enough as it is, except...

While doing all of that, some pilots have to monitor instrument readings that are projected directly into their right eye, while their left eye watches the sky to allow them to maneuver safely. Their brains must constantly process these two distinct images, which is obviously one heck of a juggling act, so they can effectively pilot the craft. It can take up to a year to learn this one skill.

Clearly, some tasks demand greater focus — you wouldn't want your heart bypass surgeon to be watching cat videos on YouTube while operating on you — but simple tasks can often be performed simultaneously to save time. Nowadays, when we are all so busy so much of the time, multitasking is often crucial to getting through what needs to be done.

Multitasking makes our lives easier. But the afterlife takes multitasking to a whole new level.

While there is debate over which gender can multitask most easily, with women usually coming out on top, there will obviously be no such limitations, nor any period to master the skill, in the afterlife. Once there, being able to multitask at a super-advanced level will be automatic. You'll be a superhero and your superpower will be multitasking!

Doesn't sound as impressive as being able to fly, to lift a car, or shoot lasers from your eyes, does it? But trust me, this is actually so much cooler.

But why multitasking? What's so important about it that we're spending so long discussing it?

Simple. Multitasking is the key to everything you ever dreamed of in the afterlife.

Remember we talked about how science has proven that some things can literally be in two places at the same time, and I suggested you could do that? This super-advanced form of multitasking is how you handle it.

In the same way you can chop vegetables while simultaneously explaining what the Fourth of July celebrates to your child, devoting part of your consciousness to one task and part to the other, so you'll be able to divide your attention in the afterlife to simultaneously experience two distinct things in two distinct places.

That is a huge concept.

Can you see the implications?

Let's look at it again to let the gravity soak in: you will be able to divide your attention to simultaneously experience two distinct and separate things in two distinct and separate places.

This means you could, say, enjoy spending time with your partner who has also passed over while simultaneously cherishing that special time when you rode your first bike with your dad. Isn't that fantastic?

If you've been paying attention, you may be frowning round about now. Why? Well, if you were only six years old when you rode that bike, how will you also spend time with your partner when you're a toddler?

This is where the beauty of the insights I'm sharing comes into its own.

In a previous chapter, we saw how time is malleable. On earth, right now, we showed that how time works can change depending on the circumstances (such as that plane and the atomic clocks). We also saw how in the afterlife, whether you believe in God or not, time works differently from here on earth.

When you consider what you want to do or who you want to do it with, your age isn't the limiting factor. In the afterlife, because time is so different, you can revisit any moment of your life, so in effect, you can be any age. You can be six years old to cycle with your dad while simultaneously being forty-two and walking hand-in-hand with your partner along a beach. That's the power of multitasking in an afterlife where time is flexible.

But it gets even better.

That "quantum superposition" I mentioned that says a thing can be in two places at once? It actually says more than that — it states a thing may be in "all" possible positions at the same time.

Yes, *all*.

That means you don't have to choose only two things to do at the same time, but as many as you'd like. Three. Twenty-six. 132... The possibilities are endless. You could:

 > revisit your son's graduation
 > snuggle up with Grandpa to watch TV
 > relive your daughter's birth (minus the screaming! This is heaven, after all.)
 > enjoy a moonlit stroll with your partner

You could have any or all of those. Or anything else you like.

While all this might sound fantastic, I'm guessing you have one or two reservations. Not least about how on earth you can keep track of five or six or even 132 other "yous" who are all doing these amazing things all at the same time.

The answer comes from a surprising source. Here's a clue — what has eight legs and lives in the ocean?

I'm guessing you know the answer, except that it hasn't answered anything, but only thrown up more questions.

So, why an octopus?

Because everyone knows what an octopus looks like, so it's the easiest way to illustrate the complex concept we're diving into.

The same as us and most creatures, an octopus has a brain that allows it to function and negotiate its environment. What you may not know is that each of an octopus's arms has its own dedicated "mini" brain. Because the octopus has so many limbs, it's far easier to outsource control of them. Each mini brain is about one-quarter as powerful as the "master" brain, so basically, the master brain gives a command to one or more of the mini brains, essentially providing an overview of what the octopus wants to do, then those mini brains work out all the fine details to move and achieve the desired result. Now, that's smart, isn't it?

But it gets better.

Each octopus arm can act with a degree of autonomy, so it can make decisions based on whatever it encounters. Yet despite this independent thinking, they are still connected to and part of the whole creature, which has ultimate control and awareness of everything that is happening. This illustrates how you can be in more than one place at the same time and act independently in each place, yet still be you.

Oh, and just because an octopus has eight arms, that doesn't mean you'll only be able to experience eight things at once – like I said, there are no limitations; the octopus is used purely because it is easy to picture, not for its number of arms.

An octopus – a real creature that everybody has heard of – proves it is possible for a being to do all manner of things at the same time, each independent of the others, yet be aware and in control of each one. If an octopus can do that on earth, imagine what you can do in the afterlife where the rules are different.

This multitasking aspect is one of the main reasons why your form will be both incorporeal and corporeal-like. An energy-like form for your "downtime" and a physical-like form for your "events" — so that hot dog tastes like a hot dog, that sunshine warms like sunshine, your mom's hug feels like a hug...

It might surprise you to learn that the two states are possible — physical and nonphysical. And guess how we know that.

Give up?

Have you ever heard of "quantum superposition?"

You have? Great!

Well, if you recall, that is part of a field called quantum mechanics, and quantum mechanics just so happens to have proved that something can be both a particle (the human body is made of particles) and a wave (light is a kind of wave).

So if an object can be both a particle and a wave, something that not long ago would have been preposterous, then in the afterlife, where some of the laws are different, there is no reason why you can't be both physical like a particle and nonphysical like a wave.

Let me guess — all this has given you more questions.

Good, because I've got more answers. Want to know how this all works and what it means for you in the afterlife? And of course, what you can do other than revisiting some aspect of your past? Then let's get to it...

Reliving the Best of Times

Okay, let's look at how you are going to use your new superpower – the power to multitask. Before we move on to all the other incredible opportunities the afterlife affords us, let's use revisiting a treasured memory to illustrate a number of important points.

If you can revisit any part of your life, to see anyone or anything, how does it work?

Today, we think of time as a straight line dotted with events. Imagine a clothesline with photographs of important events hanging off it. At one end is your birth, then a few feet in, your first day at school, further along is your first pet, then still further, your first kiss, and later, the day you graduated... That's how we see time – a continuous string of events.

If we wanted to revisit one of those times, even in our own minds, which are supposed to be under our complete control, we can only get faded impressions of it, an impression that fades more with each passing year. But even when the memory is clear, we could never visit two at the same time because that's too complex for our limited minds. To visit more than one, we'd have to leave the first, step further along the clothesline of memories, then look into another photo. Wash, rinse, repeat...

In real life, that's the only way we can relive the past because the only experience we have of time is linear — the washing line that taunts us by containing so much but letting us access so little.

However, as time works differently in the afterlife, we have a whole new way of experiencing our past.

Because this is a tricky concept to get your head around, I'll illustrate it with another "rhino" example, so don't get hung up on the practicalities.

Imagine someone has recorded every second of your life — literally — from the moment of your birth to the moment of your death. This footage has been edited into individual events (memories), all of which show on a loop on their own dedicated cable TV channel. If you want to access one, you simply click the remote control and there it is. Except instead of merely watching one TV, your multitasking superpower means you can have a bank of TVs so you can relive any number of events simultaneously and instantaneously.

This shows how the difference in the way time works means the events are no longer trapped in a linear progression for someone in the afterlife.

It is also why your superpower of multitasking is so important and where it comes into its own.

Also, these are not merely memories but interactive experiences. It's not like you are superimposed onto a video of what happened where everything is already scripted and unchangeable — you are not like Scrooge when the Ghost of Christmas Past shows him his life, but he cannot interact with it, only observe. For you, it's different. For you, you aren't an observer but the "hero" of this short story from your life, just like you were when it actually happened on earth. This is you in that event afresh, so you can see, feel, taste, hear, touch... just like you did.

Finally, you can live out the event you want to experience again and then leave, or you can extend your time there to do new things.

So, that's how you'll fill many of your days — not just reliving the highlights of your life but making them even better.

But I feel another one of your frowns coming on.

At first sight, the thought of being able to revisit cherished moments from your life seems utterly wonderful.

A first kiss.

A family celebration.

A child's birth.

How much more wonderful could heaven get?

But...

If the afterlife lasts forever — literally, forever — how many times can you relive, say, that spectacular sixth birthday party when you got the bike you'd dreamed of?

The first time will be just as moving as the first.

The second time, still great.

The third, fun, but your mind drifts, wondering about other things instead of being in the moment.

The tenth, you decide not to relive it again for a while. But eternity is longer than you'd figured and you only have so many things to relive.

The one-hundredth time...

That special memory that you cherished all through your life is suddenly a nightmare. Something to endure when you're bored rigid with nothing else to do — because eternity is long, so unbelievably long! This is pretty much how it would go, isn't it?

Whether it's a favorite food, a favorite place, a favorite song... that "favorite" status quickly wanes as it transforms from cherished to ordinary to boring to dreaded. "If I have to hear that song one more time..."

I get that. And you're right — reliving cherished moments sounds a wonderful idea if you live for a limited time, but if you live forever, and experience them over and over and over, heaven quickly becomes hell.

Except, it's heaven. So it's got you covered.

Think Afterlife Reset Button.

Whatever you wish can be as incredible as the first time — the first time you kissed your soul mate, the first time you held your child, the first time... Anything you did can feel just like the first time no matter how many times you've relived it in your afterlife.

I don't mean the memories are wiped from your mind — you still keep all those — but the sensations and emotions are renewed each time, so the way your heart raced when you saw your soul mate for the first time is the way it races every single time you relive that moment. It never pales, never gets old, never gets mundane. Every single time is just as special as the first.

But how's that possible?

Think of it like wine tasting. It sounds easy to put four glasses of wine on the table and taste each to give a verdict on your favorite. Except, once you've tasted the first glass, that taste is in your mouth, so it masks part of the second, which, in turn, also masks part of the third. By the time you reach the fourth glass, you have no real idea how much of the taste you're sensing comes only from that glass and not from the previous three.

When a professional taster wants to appreciate the differences between a number of wines, they cleanse their palate. It sounds posh and could involve some sort of scrubbing, but it's really simply eating or drinking a small amount of something that will neutralize the flavors between tastings. Olives, white bread, crackers, beer, coffee beans... all manner of things can cleanse the palate so the taste of a one-hundredth wine can be just as unique as was that of the first.

In between tastings, the taster's memory isn't wiped; they still retain all the fine details of the experience. Instead, their sense of taste is cleansed so they can appreciate the next taste sensation as the completely fresh thing that it is. This is how your Afterlife Reset Button functions — instead of cleansing the palate, you cleanse the feelings.

Suddenly, enjoying your first date with your partner for the one-thousandth time is no longer hell but the utter joy you always cherished.

But here's a thought — if the afterlife is eternal, i.e., you have unlimited time, why is it so vital that things can be done simultaneously? It's a great idea and the multitasking superpower is cool, but what's the point? If you have, literally, forever, then why can't time be linear like we've always known it so we do one thing until we've had enough, then do something else until we're bored, then find another activity and so on?

That's a good question.

Tell me, does this sound familiar:

"We are experiencing a higher call volume than usual but your call is important to us so will be answered shortly. You are currently position — twenty-seven."

When you phone a company and hear such a recorded message, does your heart sing for joy?

Or when you do your grocery shopping and push your cart toward the checkouts, if every line is a mile long, packed with carts crammed to the brim, do you leap into the air as if you've just won the lottery?

I don't know about you, but I hate waiting. I don't know anyone who does like it. So when it comes to the afterlife, do you really think there are going to be lines?

I'm guessing that one of the main reasons you want there to be an afterlife is so you can meet loved ones, whether they be friends, parents, children, relatives... Now, what if you arrive and they're all busy?

Waiting.

Is that your idea of paradise?

Of course, you could argue that they'd know you were coming, so they'd block out some time for you, but would they? Family might watch over you while you're still on earth, but how would they know you'd arrived in the afterlife? If time is linear and there's no multitasking, so they can only do one thing at a time, do you believe every single second of their afterlife should be spent watching you? What if they have other family members, should they ignore them to watch over only you? And what about their own afterlife experiences?

It's selfish to think our loved ones are going to spend decades in the afterlife doing nothing but watching us as we stumble about down here. Completely selfish. They have an afterlife to live!

This multitasking concept is the only logical way for the afterlife to work — unless, of course, your idea of paradise involves an eternity of waiting. Waiting for the partner to finish what they are doing to have time for you. Waiting for your mom to finish. Waiting for your dad, your bother, your son... even waiting for your dog! Multiple versions of you is the only solution.

This way, our families can get on with enjoying their afterlife while simultaneously keeping an eye on us so that should tragedy occur and we arrive with only a few seconds' notice, they'll be ready and waiting to greet us with open arms.

I hope that's cleared up that point for you. However, now I'm guessing you've another question — is that all you do in the afterlife? Relive things that have already happened?

Do you really think I've brought you all this way only to disappoint you now?

The Best Version of You

We've already explored how you'll have both a physical-like and a nonphysical form. What does that actually mean with relation to the physical form? For example, will you have the body you have now, flaws and all?

There is perfection in the afterlife. As you'd expect. But it isn't the "perfection" you envisage.

Popular culture portrays heaven as filled with youthful, vibrant people, all beautiful, all fit, all devoid of physical "disabilities" such as wrinkles, receding hairlines, cellulite. It's an attractive prospect. I mean, who wouldn't want the "perfect" body? If we could never achieve it on earth, whether through lack of will, money, time, commitments, or physicality, then wouldn't it be wonderful to finally know we'd have it bestowed upon us when we die?

Every society loves to do nothing better than congratulate itself on its achievements, primarily thinking how civilized and advanced it is. Further, every generation believes it is more advanced than the previous one. In this way, we believe civilization moves forward, with humanity growing not just in knowledge but in how it applies that knowledge for the betterment of all.

I have two words for you: Ukraine War.

That's how civilized and advanced we are. Six thousand years of civilization, yet here we are *still* killing each other, squabbling like petulant brats over who gets to play with which toy.

You might say it's only the Russians causing the problems (or the Chinese, or the North Koreans), but is it?

Do you and your family have good health care?

Do you always have enough quality food?

Do you have a rewarding job you love to go to?

Do you feel adequately compensated for the work you do?

Do you dream of winning money to completely change your life?

Ultimately, do you live life, or for much of the time, do you merely exist?

You see, a truly advanced and civilized people would make sure every single member of its society was healthy, fed, happy, and fulfilled.

And no, I'm not talking about communism, or legislation, or religion!

I'm talking about truly caring for our fellow man, not creating a means by which we can control or exploit him.

Of course, you could argue that mankind is slowly — so painfully slowly — evolving so we are "better" than we used to be. For example, most nations no longer tolerate slavery, most developed countries have equal rights for men and women, and most societies fight to protect and educate their young.

Wow. We're actually doing really well, aren't we? Yay for us!

And in the twentieth century, we killed almost as many people in wars as in all the other centuries combined.

Yeah, real well!

Of course, some scholars will take issue with that statistic on deaths because we have no definitive number for those that war slaughtered five hundred years ago, one thousand years ago, or whatever. Some say it could be as high as one billion, others that it's only around 150 million.

Only 150 million. Well, aren't we heroes!

Throughout human history, we have been at peace for less than ten percent of the time. Seriously, for every one hundred years that have passed, there was a war waging somewhere during ninety of those years.

And don't even get me started on what we're doing to the natural world and the climate. If the world was our pet and humanity was taken to court over how we treated it, the world would be taken away from us and found a home with decent, responsible carers, while we'd be banned from ever owning another one for the rest of our lives.

We are in an abusive relationship, but the victim has no one rushing to their aid.

The root of the problem is that, in order to truly advance, we don't have to change what people do but change what they think. How do you legislate for that?

You can't.

We need a fundamental shift in how we view the world and our place in it, but we have no way of bringing it about.

Now, I'm not railing against consumerism — I like to buy stuff just as much as the next guy — but we encourage a throwaway culture and love nothing more than sweeping ecological problems under the carpet. Talk about dumb.

Now, I know what you're thinking — this fascinating exploration of the afterlife has just taken a horrendous turn into some left-wing, bleeding heart, tree-hugging diatribe.

Yes, I can see how it might appear like that. But trust me, I'm going somewhere with this. Somewhere important.

So, what's all this got to do with the afterlife?

It's to do with mindset. Or more specifically, how our minds evolve over the centuries to push humanity forward. You see, our minds are the key.

Unfortunately, despite the fact we have developed a sophisticated language, have implemented laws to protect every member of society, have created computers and cars and planes and the internet to open up the world and knowledge so everyone everywhere can learn and grow and flourish...

It doesn't work.

While the material things we love to cram our lives with have evolved, *we* haven't. At least not enough.

Fortunately, the afterlife will be different.

So will each of us become the "best version" of ourselves in the afterlife?

Yes.

But that doesn't necessitate being physically perfect. At least not the Hollywood version of perfection — men with chiseled abs, women with supermodel figures, and the like. The afterlife's version of perfection resides inside us, not outside. People can be bald, be scarred, be old, be overweight, be disabled... we just won't see it. To us, they'll just *be* a person. A human *being*. As they should be now but sadly all too often aren't.

Our mindset will be perfect, so everything external to us doesn't have to be.

But what happens if a person only has, say, one leg due to an accident, or was born blind? Will they "struggle" for eternity?

Again, "struggle" is often in the eye of the beholder. It's a mindset thing.

Will every person who was born blind, or became blind over their lifetime, have sight "forced" upon them? Or will they get the choice?

This is the afterlife, where freedom and choice are paramount. If a blind person wants sight, fine, but if they don't, that's fine, too.

Like I said, our mindset must change. We don't assume what would be best for another person but allow them to choose, and once they have, we don't judge. Judgments cause so many problems in our life on earth that this tendency has no place in the afterlife.

But this idea extends further.

This is the afterlife, so you won't have the same kind of feelings and appetites that you have on earth — there won't be envy, greed, hate, impatience, intolerance, ambition...

Take jealousy, for example. Why won't it exist?

Why would anyone be jealous when they have access to virtually anything they can dream of?

Just like time and place, emotion is rewired. Of course there'll still be positive emotions, such as love for friends and family, but there won't be negative emotions because the triggers that drove such things simply won't exist.

How can you be envious of someone for living in a mansion and driving a flashy car when you can create such "toys" for your amusement any time you like?

This new mindset will make the afterlife easier for you and for everybody with whom you come into contact. Of course, the benefit will be mutual.

So, you and I will be as perfect as we want to be.

And we'll accept others for being as perfect as they want to be, too.

And it isn't only the mindset that will create a perfect environment.

Because our consciousness can interact with other consciousnesses in the afterlife, there is no need for language as we know it. We can still choose to use language if we so wish, for example, when we interact with loved ones, but it's not necessary. Language is rich and vibrant, but endless problems are caused when an innocent thought is translated into words that, to the listener, communicates something quite different from what was intended. You won't believe the problems that have been created between me and Kasia when I have "said" one thing, but she's "heard" something else. Especially as English isn't her first language. While she's fluent, occasionally, there is vocabulary, nuance, or simply poor word choice that can all throw a wrench in the works.

Misunderstandings won't happen in the afterlife the way they do on earth because we will be connected at a higher level, making language redundant. This doesn't mean you will be able to read another person's mind, but more a case of you and them consensually sharing thoughts. Thus ending the problem of the vagaries of language.

So, everyone is their version of perfection, and confusion is a thing of the past. Does the afterlife have any other treasures awaiting us or is that it?

I'm so pleased you asked...

Animals, Friends, and Everything in the Afterlife

In a moment, we'll explore a glorious snapshot of what an average "day" in the afterlife might look like for you. However, there's something absolutely crucial that we need to address first. Something I'm guessing you might have thought about or, in your excitement at what awaits us, maybe has never crossed your mind, but it should!

You see, we've spent most of this book talking about *you*. What the afterlife will be like for *you*. What form *you* will have in the afterlife. What *you* will do in the afterlife.

But there's a serious element missing. In fact, trillions of elements missing.

Trillions?

You'd think we'd have noticed if such a gigantic number of things were missing, so what could they possibly be that we've overlooked them?

Simple.

Everything else that's in the afterlife *with you*.

For example, while it will be wonderful for me to see family I've lost, I also yearn to see the animals who have shared my life. I'm sure many people reading this will ache to see their beloved companions too. So will our furry friends (or bald or scaly...) be waiting for us in the afterlife, tails wagging, tongues licking, longing to curl up in our laps or fetch a ball?

Many ancient religions believed that humans weren't the only creature to have a soul. For example, they believed trees had spirits, as did mountains, even plain old rocks. What would you say if I told you that was true?

"Woo-woo alert! Quick, run. RUN!"

Don't panic. Sit back and get comfy so I can explain.

I said "if" I told you that was true, didn't I? I didn't claim outright that it was. But could it be?

According to the US Department of State, in Japan, right now, around ninety million people follow Shintoism. The Shinto religion holds that anything can have a spirit, from waterfalls to rocks, sunshine to hedgehogs. Ninety million people. Here in the West, we'd have to go back centuries to find even a fraction of that number of people who believe a tree has a spirit. Today, we're way too sophisticated to fall for mumbo-jumbo like that, aren't we?

Well...

What if we're wrong and the Shinto followers are right?

And this is where we run into two major problems when discussing this topic:

> What is consciousness?

> Are the soul and consciousness the same thing?

We've already explored the latter — we simply do not know if the soul and consciousness are one and the same.

As for what consciousness is? The problem is threefold.

Firstly, there is an issue in how we define consciousness. The problem here is that if we define it too narrowly, we limit the world around us and, in so doing, deprive ourselves of the answers we crave.

For example, not many years ago, the world's greatest minds all agreed that the only self-aware species in the universe was mankind. As science evolved, we didn't become smarter as a species, merely more capable, and we realized how wrong we were and that there were indeed other species that were self-aware. So, the first issue we must deal with is how we define consciousness, which is a subject in itself as it is in a constant state of flux, making it all the harder to produce solid answers.

The second big issue was hinted at above — how we detect consciousness. For centuries we denied the existence of any consciousness comparable to ours anywhere in the animal kingdom. Then we discovered how wrong we were because we developed more accurate and more reliable methods of evaluating how other creatures processed the world. Those creatures didn't change — our perception of them did.

Unfortunately, though our investigative techniques have improved, they are still in their infancy in the grand scheme of giving us definitive answers on what is and what isn't conscious and self-aware. Research is ongoing but is struggling with both the definition issue and the detection issue. However, things get even trickier.

The third problem with consciousness is that the further a species is away from our own, the harder it is to quantify and qualify whatever consciousness it may have.

There are some things we do know, however.

When we look at the facts, we know most animals have some level of consciousness, even if it isn't on a comparable level to ours. Further, we used to like to class ourselves as the superior species because we were self-aware. That was a great divider between humans and the rest of the natural world.

Scientists everywhere agreed that we were the only species to possess self-awareness.

And guess what — all those scientists were wrong.

Today, we still aren't sure how many species are self-aware, but we know ours isn't the only one. To date, as is the case with much of our scientific knowledge, we don't have a definitive list of creatures that possess consciousness and self-awareness, but it's been widely accepted for decades that some animals have both. The list includes, for example, chimpanzees, orangutans, dolphins, orcas, magpies, and elephants.

Identifying self-awareness and consciousness in these creatures was a major discovery. Not least because it means we need to ensure our moral compass is pointing in the right direction when we consider how we interact with species that have a similar level of consciousness to us. For example, if they experience not just physical pain but emotional pain, obviously we must treat them better than a species that doesn't suffer emotionally. (That doesn't mean we can be as cruel as we like to species that are not self-aware, but that's a whole other area that is far beyond the scope of this book.)

Did you notice anything special about that list of animals above? Chimpanzees, orangutans, dolphins, orcas, magpies, and elephants?

I'm sure you did, even if it was only on a subconscious level. That list includes two distinct classes of vertebrate animal: mammals and birds. If consciousness and self-awareness can originate not just in different species but in different classifications of species, who's to say where else they might reside? It proves that consciousness and self-awareness are *not* unique to us but far, far more prevalent than we ever dreamed possible.

And just to further hammer that nail into the coffin of mankind's superiority...

There *are* many, many more species that are self-aware and we simply don't know it. Not because the animals themselves aren't smart enough, but because *we* aren't. We simply aren't smart enough to invent a reliable means of testing them. It is *our* failing, not *theirs*.

Now, hold on to your socks because this could blow them off!

Some researchers believe they've discovered evidence to prove that bees have a primitive consciousness and are self-aware, in a similar way to how we are. In experiments, bees have demonstrated emotions akin to optimism, frustration, playfulness, and fear. They've also shown that they can recognize different people's faces and that they have long-term memories.

Wow!

But there's more...

Other researchers believe they've proved that some species of ant are self-aware by having individuals take the mirror test, which is designed to see if a creature recognizes its own reflection, and therefore itself. This is a hugely important test, though it does have its limitations, so it is not definitive.

Further, it's been recently discovered that some species of spider dream when they sleep. Though more research is needed, this suggests a far higher level of consciousness in arachnids than previously believed. But when it's difficult to test a chimpanzee — a species with which we have such a huge amount in common — how can we go about testing a spider, which in comparison to humans and chimps is so different that it's like something from a different planet? Do you see the problem we face?

A creature such as a chimp is easy because, fundamentally, they are so similar to us — mammal, two arms, two legs, a head with mouth, nose, two ears, two eyes. We understand their physicality and their psychology because we can see they aren't that different from our own, so we've studied them for decades. This makes it far easier to develop tests, because we can imagine how their brain may process things. It also makes it much easier to interpret the results because we know how we process such things, and because of the similarities in our two species, we can transpose our processing onto theirs. If there's a match, then we've proven something.

But a spider with eight legs, eight eyes, no fathomable emotions, no discernible societal structure, no understandable mannerisms… how can we put ourselves in their world enough to judge what test will be appropriate and give valid results? And even if we could design a test, how would we then interpret the results as we struggle to understand much of their world as they do ours? Getting reliable results, and interpreting them correctly, thus becomes a huge headache.

But it doesn't stop with those species. Other researchers have found that some species of fish can recognize themselves in a mirror, which, again, is one of the main tests to prove self-awareness. Some fish can also recognize their owner's face.

You're not going to believe this, but there's more…

Snakes.

While the class of reptiles is probably the least researched of the lot, it's been proposed that snakes can identify things that have their scent on them, i.e., instead of recognizing themselves in a mirror, they recognize their own smell on something as opposed to that of another snake. They've also been observed to show a preference for which other snakes they spend time with, i.e., which snakes are "their friends." There isn't as much research conducted into reptiles, so of all the classes of vertebrates, these and amphibians are least known. But for a snake to have preferences over who it spends its time with, that surely suggests there's far more going on in that little head than we ever dreamed there could be.

Bees, ants, and spiders are classified as arthropods, fish are, unsurprisingly, classified as fish, and snakes are reptiles. If all this research proves correct, that will give us species of mammals, birds, arthropods, reptiles, and fish that are self-aware. That's five of animal, including four of the five vertebrate classes, which are what most of us would think of as the "main" classes. Where is this going to end?

But as an entire book could be written about self-awareness testing, not to mention the ethical implications of finding that some insects and arachnids are self-aware, we better move on.

Okay, so it is scientifically accepted that some species other than humans possess consciousness and self-awareness. But there have to be limits, right? I mean, a tree? Come on!

Would we be right to dismiss such an idea as preposterous? Or is it that we are not as sophisticated as we believe? Is that an example of another species where it is *we* who have failed again because we just aren't smart enough to develop a testing model?

We've already discussed how consciousness and the soul are, if not one and the same, inextricably entwined, so what would happen if science discovered that things other than most living creatures actually have consciousness?

The *Oxford Dictionary of Psychology* defines consciousness as "characterized by the experience of perceptions, thoughts, feelings, awareness of the external world, and often in humans (but not necessarily in other animals) self-awareness."

How could we apply those criteria to a tree? A tree can obviously perceive things. In July 2022, I witnessed trees "perceiving" the world around them — in both England and Poland, I saw what is termed a false autumn. The trees had suffered so much as a result of the summer's excessive heat and lack of water that they went into survival mode — they dropped their leaves in July as opposed to October/November.

Further, it's long since been established that trees can communicate when they "perceive" a threat, for example, a leaf-eating caterpillar. In such instances, a tree releases chemicals to warn other nearby plants.

That's the first criterion fulfilled. How about the second? Thoughts?

Hmmm... sorry, trees, but I don't think so. At least not in the way contemporary science would recognize.

Number three: feelings?

Again, not in the way contemporary science would recognize.

And the last — awareness of the external world?

Again, no.

Yes, trees can sense things — like an attack by a parasite — but that's not really "feeling" or "thinking" or even "awareness." The tree is obviously aware of something happening, but it isn't aware of the external world in the way an insect, a dog, or a person is.

So, it looks like it's safe to say that trees, and by extension, most plants, do not possess consciousness.

So how about things like rocks and water?

Give me a break.

Wait...

This is going to blow your mind. Seriously!

Scratch all that about trees. You see, thanks to our old friend quantum mechanics, researchers have recently made what could be a startling discovery — it is *possible* that everything has a degree of consciousness, even inanimate objects. Research is ongoing, but the possibility is there.

So let's put that in the simplest terms — scientists cannot categorically say whether a rock does or does not have some level of consciousness.

It sounds absolutely crazy, doesn't it? Which is why many, many respected scientists are arguing against the idea. But that isn't stopping equally respected scientists from researching the possibility.

What does this mean for us?

If consciousness and the soul are as interconnected as they appear, and the soul is the part of you that goes into the afterlife, then if everything has consciousness, everything goes into the afterlife.

This won't come as any surprise to pet lovers who have long believed their beloved companions go to the rainbow bridge to await their reunion. Pet lovers know their companions have a consciousness without any test being necessary because they've witnessed firsthand how their little friend has a personality. And nothing can have a personality without a consciousness. So, this is how all our animal friends will be waiting for us to join them. What a day that will be! [Big smile at that thought!]

Everything possessing some degree of consciousness is a weird idea, yes, but when you think about it, it's the only idea that makes sense — you'd expect to find trees, waterfalls, rocks, flowers, and everything else in the afterlife, so what better way for them to get there than through having a level of consciousness?

Level. That is the crucial word in that sentence.

Obviously a tree in your garden doesn't have the consciousness of a spider that lives in it, which doesn't have the consciousness of your dog, which doesn't have the consciousness of you or me.

Level. I think of it like sugar in coffee. I like one and a half spoonfuls. I've known people to have two, some three or even more.

So think of consciousness in terms of the amount of sugar in a coffee. For example, people are three spoonfuls. Chimpanzees and the other animals with self-awareness are two and a half. Cats and dogs? A solid two. Gradually, we assess the entire world, both animate and inanimate, right down through the mammals, fish, insects, plants... to that good old rock.

How many spoonfuls for a rock? I think one solitary grain of sugar would suffice, don't you?

When you think about it, we shouldn't really be surprised if we do discover that everything possess at least a single grain of sugary consciousness. You see, everything around us, the entire material world in which we live, is made of "stuff." This stuff is what scientists call matter. It can be living (animate) or not living (inanimate). It can be solid like rock, invisible and untouchable like air, or something in between like water. Everything is made of matter — you, me, your dog, a tree, a bicycle...

But how is it all made of the same stuff when it's all so different?

Well, is it different? You'll be amazed to hear that it is not as different as you may at first think.

To simplify things, let's say you have a pile of metal, plastic, glass, and rubber. What can you do with that? You could build a car. Great. Or, using different proportions of those materials in different combinations, you could build a TV. Same "stuff," different result.

Matter works the same way. Literally everything is made of the same "stuff," but just in different proportions and different combinations. And the pile of materials you use to build it is far bigger. You've no doubt heard of things like oxygen, iron, gold, hydrogen, and mercury — those are some of the building blocks of all matter and are called elements. And unlike our pile, where we only had four materials to build a car, there are 118 elements, so the number of combinations is huge, which explains why the world, and the universe, are filled with so many different and amazing things.

But get this — even though all of these elements are different, they're actually made up of the same things themselves, which are atoms. For a long, long time, scientists believed that the atom was the smallest thing possible. Later they discovered they were wrong.

You see, when you cut an atom open and look inside, you find that too is made of other things — electrons, protons, and neutrons. It was then decided that these were the smallest things possible.

And guess what? That was wrong, too.

You see, if you cut protons and neutrons open, you discover they're made up of quarks and gluons. And all that "stuff" is held in place mainly by two forces: an electromagnetic force and what scientists have unimaginatively called the "strong force" (come on, guys, you could try a bit harder).

Now, before we continue, a quick question — did you notice anything familiar in that last paragraph?

No?

How about "electromagnetic"? We've come across that before, haven't we?

But don't worry if you don't recall where, because we'll circle back to it.

And don't worry about all this terminology because it's not important. What we need to focus on is that all atoms — *all atoms* — are made up of electrons, protons, and neutrons, with the latter two being composed of quarks and gluons. Essentially, they are all made of the same "stuff" and held together by the same forces. Whether it's gold, oxygen, helium, molybdenum, zinc, promethium, silver... they're *all* made of the same stuff.

You, me, a tree, a porcupine, a cloud, a rock, a dinosaur... all made of atoms, which are all made of exactly the same stuff held together in exactly the same way.

Yep, we and everything in existence are made of the same stuff.

Now, the 2020 Nobel laureate in physics is an expert in quantum mechanics, which, if you recall, is the science of subatomic particles, such as electrons, protons, neutrons, quarks, and gluons. He believes there's a connection between quantum mechanics and consciousness.

When *everything* is made of the same stuff, and that stuff could be responsible for consciousness, it isn't that much of a stretch to believe that everything could, therefore, have a level of consciousness, even a rock.

For centuries, some forms of religion and philosophy have told us that we are all connected. Not just in that we live on the earth together, but on a much, much deeper level. We've known for some time that we are all made of the same "stuff," but now it appears that connection could be far more real than we ever imagined possible.

When you consider the soul takes an energy-like form that could be akin to electromagnetic radiation, this connection, this concept that everything has consciousness, shouldn't come as anything of a surprise because everything, at a subatomic level, is held together by an electromagnetic force.

Apart from its other implications, it is this connection we have to everyone and everything that makes it possible for us to manifest whatever we wish in the afterlife.

And if you think this concept of consciousness is too far out to have any truth in it, you'll be surprised to hear that it is quite tame compared to others. Some theories of reality take consciousness to an extreme level. For example, one suggests that there is no such thing as matter but that only consciousness exists. Then there's the theory that's been around for a while and suggests we are little more than digital-like creations living in a digital-like universe — in other words, we are no more than a sophisticated video game. However, as such theories are very much on the fringes of science and philosophy, we won't explore them.

We've covered a heck of a lot in this chapter, so while we could delve deeper into this fascinating subject, let's cut to the chase.

If everything has a level of consciousness, so everything can appear in the afterlife, what does it mean for us?

For me, it means I'll have a huge smile on my face because my pets will be waiting for me! What's it mean for you?

An Average Day in the Afterlife

I bet you're thrilled that you'll be able not just to be reunited with your loved ones but to relive the most treasured moments of your life — but I'm also betting you're wondering if that's all there is as it's all we've discussed so far.

No, of course there's more.

You'll be free to meet new people, too. The afterlife will have a community and opportunities for you to mingle, learn new things, experience new activities, and discover new interests. Your imagination is the only limitation. That doesn't mean you'll reach the afterlife and automatically be able to befriend Elvis, or skydive with Queen Elizabeth II, or compose a concerto with Mozart.

Just because you'll be the "best" you, doesn't mean you'll automatically become a master of everything and have access to everyone.

Take music. If you and everyone else can compose like Lennon and McCartney, or sing like Beyoncé, or play guitar like Hendrix, then who and what can ever be special? If everyone is gifted, no one is gifted.

Plus, part of the pleasure of learning something new is in the actual *learning* — the resulting progression from completely useless to fair to reasonable to good to accomplished. Take that journey away and there is little point in achieving anything.

For example, if I could receive $1 million next year in one of two ways, which do you think I'd go for?

Option 1

I'm simply handed the money after winning the lottery. No skill. No achievement. No journey. Just money.

Option 2

I pour my soul into writing a book. Once published, its sales are dismal. But a small group of readers love it and talk about it online. Nonstop! Word spreads. And sales grow. Then a celebrity is photographed carrying a copy. Sales skyrocket overnight. Finally, a New York publisher offers me a $1 million advance for the rights.

The second option obviously involves considerable work, and then waiting, and doubting, and fearing failure... Talk about nerve-wracking. But the payoff? Oh boy, for a writer, you don't get a better journey than that one!

So even in the afterlife, the journey undertaken to achieve something is crucial.

However, this doesn't mean that everything will be a struggle. A level of proficiency in virtually anything will come relatively easily, and progression will be accelerated, but total mastery at the "flick of a switch," so to speak, will not happen. It would be pointless because it would be joyless.

As for meeting celebrities...

We've already talked about mindset and how most of the negative emotions we know on earth will vanish. That means that "celebrity" won't hold the fascination for us that it does now. We won't be envious of their talent, fame, wealth, or anything, so their status will diminish. Of course, we'll still appreciate the gifts they gave during their lifetime and any they continue to give, but the fixation that many people have with celebrities and the celebrity lifestyle will not exist.

This will obviously make the afterlife easier for celebrities, too.

Added to that is the fact that this is their afterlife, so they may not want to make any new friends or waste a single moment meeting strangers when they could devote all of their energy to enjoying the friends and family they have or embarking on new interests and adventures. This is not them being snooty, merely them doing exactly what you want to do — enjoy the afterlife, which involves not suffering hassle.

So let's explore what you can do in the afterlife. To help, I have a crazy image for you to get your head around that, if you can visualize it, makes all this fit together in one magical picture.

Remember our octopus friend from a few chapters back? Imagine you're an octopus — yep, eight arms, the lot. Except you don't live in the ocean, because this is the afterlife, but in a luxurious mansion that has a beautiful marble lobby with stone columns and a sweeping staircase. All around you, both upstairs and downstairs, are doorways. Except the doors don't open to other rooms, they open to all the events from your past that you want to relive or to new adventures you want to enjoy. To experience them, you simply sit in the lobby and reach an arm through the appropriate doorway. Then, you multitask, your various arms using their mini brains to experience whatever is beyond the doors you've chosen to open, each doing so independently and yet with your full awareness and control.

Each arm is a "you." And you aren't limited to the eight that an octopus has, but however many you need to be able to do all the things you want to do. So every moment, you are free to explore as many or as few new experiences or events from your past as you wish. All simultaneously.

But the doors don't only go to all these different places in space, but *seemingly* to different places in time, so each arm experiences what is beyond the door in a time of its own with your age adjusting appropriately. This is how you can revisit your past to feel both the childhood glee of riding a bike with your dad and the adult exhilaration of the first kiss with your life partner.

The octopus is just a visual aid — you don't become one in the afterlife, so don't panic! This is merely to help you picture what's possible. Eight arms is illustrative too — you could choose to do only one thing at a time or five or twenty. This is the beauty of it.

You're probably thinking that revisiting the past sounds incredible, but is that all there is to the afterlife? Surely there should be more, right? I've mentioned you can do, literally, anything, but how does that actually work?

Reliving cherished moments is only one of the five elements that make up what you'll do in the afterlife. So, let's look at what else you can do by considering the other four options.

Firstly, as a conscious being, you can bask in the light of other such beings.

Secondly, you can watch over your loved ones who are still on earth.

Thirdly, you can explore history.

Fourthly, you get to meet new people.

Finally, there are whole worlds for you to explore and "live" in, if you so wish.

Let's look at that consciousness option first.

This is where you drift in an ocean of souls. In an energy-like form, you bask in a sea of consciousness, warmed, buoyed, nourished, and above all, loved. A sense of being loved and of deserving that love, of belonging, is all around and unending.

It's a cocoon of love. A harmony. A connection to something greater than you, and yet, something that *is* you.

Think of your life now. Think of when you've just woken up in bed on a day you don't have to go to work. You haven't opened your eyes yet, and you're *so* warm and cozy, so you simply lie, relishing the moment. Peaceful and snug. You feel like you could lie like that forever — cocooned in contentment.

Or maybe you meditate and delight in that feeling of serenity that washes over you.

Or maybe you can afford to pamper yourself at a spa and love nothing more than to drift away as you lie in a flotation tank or as a masseuse massages the world out of existence.

Now, multiply that peace and contentment a thousandfold and that's the bliss of wallowing in the ocean of consciousnesses. Except no kids run in and jump on the bed, no text message alert drags you out of your bliss, no dog whines it needs a pee... it's unending. Unless you wish it to end.

But when it's just little old you in a vast ocean of billions, won't you get lost? Engulfed by so many, won't you lose "you"? Won't you become so overwhelmed that it's like you don't matter, so you don't exist?

Think of a cup of coffee with milk and sugar. The water, coffee, sugar, and milk were all individual entities at one point, but in a drink, they blend so each "touches," "experiences," and "interacts" with the others. Yet, each is still present and identifiable — as is obvious to, say, anyone who loves two sugars and sipped from a drink that hasn't been stirred. Even when the sugar is dissolved, its presence is still felt. Just like yours will be.

This is the "cosmic soup" where souls reside together. Each capable of mingling with endless other souls, yet each remaining unique, just like sugar mixed in a beverage.

So what happens when you choose this drifting in the ocean of consciousnesses to end?

If you still have loved ones on earth — a partner, children, parents, or whoever — you can watch over them.

This is why the concepts we've discussed about time and being in two places simultaneously are so important.

Firstly, no matter how much you love your children, I doubt you'd want to spend fifty or sixty years doing nothing else but glued to their every move. Apart from anything, what would you do for the eight hours a day they sleep? Seriously, while it might sound like a good idea, a week or two of relentlessly watching over them and you'll be going nuts.

Secondly, most parents have more than one child, so how do you decide who to watch over if you can't be in two places at once? Imagine if you could only be in one place and something happened to your other child while you weren't watching. You'd never forgive yourself. Even though you can't interfere but only watch, you'd still hate the fact that you weren't there, so your child had to endure the ordeal alone.

So, versions of you, your "octopus arms," can be permanently watching over your children, whether you have one, two, ten… it doesn't matter. You can create however many "yous" needed to fulfill whatever "watching-over" duties you like.

And that brings us to the third option for what you can do in the afterlife — explore history.

In an earlier chapter, we looked at how we'll be able to see the whole of history, forward and backward. The crucial word there is *see* — we won't be able to interfere with past events or influence future events; we'll only be able to watch them unfold.

Think of it like the ultimate streaming service. Like Netflix on steroids. Simply by thinking about it, you'll be able to watch any event from the whole of time. Or simply pop to a random date to see what's happening.

So, whether it's witnessing the construction of the Great Pyramid of Giza in 2560 BCE, watching Leonardo da Vinci paint the Mona Lisa in sixteenth-century Florence, or jumping into 2085 and cheering at Super Bowl **CXIX**... the choice is yours.

I know one thing, we'll never be able to complain there's nothing to watch ever again!

The fourth option is simply to meet new people in one of the communal areas where anyone can go to simply mingle. For example, you could enjoy a lakeside hike and stop to skim pebbles over the water. A guy ambles over and chats. You share a joke and then have a friendly competition to see who can get the most bounces out of three throws. It ends in a draw. You share a picnic on the shore, then, together, stroll farther, basking in the glorious tranquility. You tell your new friend a little about your old life. And he casually shares something of his and you discover that this ordinary guy who has befriended you is none other than Michelangelo, one of the greatest artists to ever live.

Not every encounter will be with someone famous, but they will all be equally warm, satisfying, and natural. Souls will be drawn to others with whom they have a kinship, so there will be no social awkwardness or needing to "try." Just an easiness in each other's company. And a warm sense of belonging.

The last option of the five is the most complex because it involves new interests and new adventures in completely new worlds that you've created.

One problem with many conceptions of heaven is that they make it almost the same as our world, but just bigger, more beautiful, and all around better. People live in luxurious places, eat fabulous food, do incredible things... but all in a world that, in many ways, is identical to ours.

This is understandable because this world is the only one we've ever known. Unfortunately, that concept of heaven is deeply flawed.

In that version of heaven, people can work, doing the jobs they've always dreamed of doing, which give them the fulfillment they've always dreamed of. So we all get to be sports stars, or movie icons, or famous authors, or rock gods... and live in a fabulous mansion, dine in exquisite restaurants, frolic on golden beaches...

Except, who cleans the toilet?

Seriously.

In this version of heaven, who cleans the toilet in your luxury mansion?

Or do you really think there are vast hordes of people who can't wait to get to heaven so they can do *that* dream job?

And somehow, I don't think that's the purpose God had in mind when He created angels, though I might be wrong!

After all, He is said to work in mysterious ways.

Obviously, should people need a toilet in heaven, then they'll be magic toilets that somehow clean themselves.

Just like the streets will magically clean themselves of litter, fallen leaves, and what have you.

Just like the dishes in those fancy restaurants we visit will all magically clean themselves.

Anything inanimate will obviously magically take care of itself. This is heaven, right? So it's all done. Somehow.

So, no need for people to get down on their hands and knees to scrub a toilet. Fine. That's that issue resolved.

But is it?

It's all well and good that inanimate objects are magically renewed in some way, but in that restaurant, who brings us that food? The eighteen-year-old who has dreamed all their life of getting to heaven to wait on tables?

So the food magically appears on the table, too. And drinks at the bar. And planes fly themselves, just like taxis drive themselves.

In this version of the afterlife, there can be no service jobs or any position where one person needs to work at something they wouldn't have freely chosen to do in life even if they were rich. Here, people magically conjure up whatever they need, making it completely unlike life on earth, completely alien.

Plus, with no menial labor, every single person is free to be a rock star, or a movie star, or a sports star...

Invariably, people dream of being a star because of the accolades associated with it, which usually bring material wealth. We crave glamour because our society has bred that into us — we see a glamorous lifestyle as a sign of success. But is it?

Do rock stars and sports stars never get divorced, never turn to drugs, never feel depressed?

Contentment and material wealth are two wildly contrasting things. They aren't mutually exclusive, but one *never* depends on the other.

On top of that, what is the only reason that anyone would want to work in heaven?

To achieve something, right?

And how do you achieve something notable if everyone else is achieving exactly the same thing in exactly the same way? If you're a songwriter, what makes your "masterpiece" different from the millions of other "masterpieces" churned out every second by the millions of other souls with the whim to do so?

The simple answer is that you can't achieve anything notable that way. If everyone is a rock star, then that word *star* becomes meaningless.

These ideas of heaven simply cannot work. They wouldn't create a heaven that we would recognize — conjuring everything up like that might work in Wizard Heaven, but not the heaven we believe in. Conjuring this, conjuring that — it's more like something out of Harry Potter than an afterlife we'd recognize.

So, how does it really work?

Simple.

If we so wish, we create infinite worlds in which to live and work. If you believe in God, then it's He who creates them. If you don't believe, then it's the collective power of the ocean of souls that manifests things into being.

A unique world is created for every person. Other people can visit, of course, but they each have their own world (which you can visit). And because of the multiple "yous" aspect, you and they can spend as much time as you like in visiting each other.

But back to your world. In your world, you aren't king or anything like that, but it is a utopian version of life on earth — no poverty, no disease, no suffering.

Now you must be wondering why on earth anyone would want to live in their own world all by themselves with just the occasional visitor. Yes?

Here's the secret — they don't live by themselves. Though the world isn't populated with other people, it *is* populated.

The closest thing on earth that it could be compared to is a never-ending virtual reality video game of infinite size. In your personal created world, you can go anywhere, do anything, interact with anyone.

But this isn't virtual in the sense we understand it. It's as real to us as this world we live in now. Our fellow citizens aren't merely pixels but are indistinguishable from real beings, i.e., physical. Right now, you're probably picturing either the jerky automatons you saw at a theme park decades ago or *Westworld*.

No, this is vastly more sophisticated.

But where sentient robots in the real world would throw up all kinds of ethical and moral dilemmas, not least around slavery and the rights such beings should be entitled to, in the afterlife, there are no such issues. These beings are only "real" in so far as they populate your virtual world. The moment you leave that world, they cease to exist.

It's like super AI (artificial intelligence). An ordinary video game can have the most incredible interactivity with the characters it creates, yet the moment the console is turned off, those characters are no more. They don't go on existing without you present and playing the game, therefore, there is no moral quandary over their role in their world. This created world acts like that.

Does this make the characters any less real to interact with?

No. When in that world with them, they are as real as you and me.

And in case you don't think it's possible to form a true friendship with something akin to an AI person – this is happening right now, here on earth. In 2023, AI has made huge advances, one result being that people are forming *real* relationships with AI chatbots. Virtual companionship could easily become a boom industry.

But as a whole book could be devoted to AI and our relationship with it, not least if machines ever develop what we'd call consciousness, we'll move on.

I'm guessing you might be wondering why the afterlife goes to all this trouble when it could simply fill the world with real people.

For the reasons specified earlier – who wants to spend eternity cleaning toilets?

But also, because real people in the afterlife have their own desires that might not gel with yours. For example, imagine you want to create music with your best friend. In the world you create for this, you already have a level of proficiency with whatever musical instrument you choose (guitar, voice, keyboards, etc.), but you aren't a master – where would be the sense of achievement if you were a new Beyoncé with the snap of your fingers?

In this created world, you and your friend start writing music, then play in small bars and coffee shops. And people like you. *Really* like you.

You start to get a name. And the more you play together, the more you write, the better you become, so the more attention you receive.

Soon, you have a following of loyal fans.

Tiny gigs turn into supporting acts for major bands, and then you get a big break — you're offered your first TV appearance.

Except your writing partner decides that's as far as they want to take things, so leaves the band to go back to their own created world, leaving you high and dry.

That isn't how heaven is supposed to work, is it? Crushing disappointment isn't supposed to be part of the deal.

But your partner is a real person with their own needs and desires, their own right to choose how they spend their time in the afterlife. If they want to end things there, they have every right to do so. That means it's the end of your dream. Suddenly heaven doesn't feel so heavenly.

Now, what if instead of starting a band with your real best friend, you started it with a new friend — one of the AI-like people who populate your world? These people have desires and motivations too, but their purpose in the afterlife is not to have their own dreams but to ensure that you live yours. In this scenario, the band doesn't break up, you get your TV break, and your music is enjoyed by millions.

It's important to note that these AI people aren't slaves who are only there to do your bidding; they exist to populate the world, and to add atmosphere and a sense of realism. They don't bow down before you as if you're a god to them, but neither do they block your whatever journey you undertake in this created world.

Think of it like this — this world is not filled with never-ending yes-men but with the kind of pleasant, helpful and cooperative people we are sometimes fortunate enough to meet here on earth. Sadly, such people often seem far too few, but in any created world, it's all you're going to meet. These AI people have their own agendas and needs, just like real people, which makes them as real as they can be, but their agendas and needs never conflict with yours, so you are guaranteed a happy ending to whatever adventure you undertake.

Of course, there are challenges in this world. It's not a cakewalk to do whatever you like, because, again, where would be the sense of achievement in that? If you want to succeed, you'll have to work at whatever your dream is and thereby gain self-respect, confidence, and mastery.

And that's what this aspect of the afterlife is about — achievement. Not material success. Not accolades. It's about the fulfillment, pleasure, and contentment that achieving a goal brings. Whether that's mastering a musical instrument, hiking the Amazon, or building a lakeside house. The only limits are your imagination and your will to see the adventure through.

Naturally, you can abandon anything at any time. Just because you've started a project doesn't mean you have to see it through to its ultimate conclusion. For example, you might be content to master the piano but never perform publicly, gaining your sense of achievement from composing an original work that only you hear, or by performing breathtaking renditions of the works of Chopin with your only listener being your cat.

Achievement takes many forms. And it's always your choice.

Plus, just like a video game, you can choose how difficult you want achieving your goal to be. As we've discussed, achieving something too easily takes away its true value, so instead of obstacles being problematic to your journey, they actually add to it.

Okay, now that's all clear, let's have a look at a typical "day" in the afterlife (though "days" don't strictly exist unless you create a world in which you want them to). This is where the "octopus you" that we discussed earlier comes into its own, and all of those independent arms do their thing. So, what do all the versions of you do?

You #1 — Having a fascination for history, you visit the Boston Tea Party in December 1773. You gaze on as the Sons of Liberty throw forty-six tons of tea, which would be worth around $2 million today, into the harbor in protest at the taxes imposed by the British Empire.

You #2 — Being a big sports fan, you travel back to 1989 to admire Michael Jordan's "The Shot" — the most legendary shot in basketball history.

You #3 — Your daughter is still on earth. This version of you spends every moment of every day watching over her.

You #4 — Having always dreamed of writing a book, you create a world in which you spend a year writing one, mainly in a local coffee shop or on your beachfront veranda. It's well-received, so you adapt it into a low-budget movie, which you direct. Audiences love it.

You #5 — In 2072, you watch your great-great-grandson participate in the Rome Olympics. He gets knocked out in the heats for the 100 meters, but as you watch the 200 meters, you cry with joy when he tears across the finish line to win a silver medal.

You #6 — You enjoy a lazy stroll through a lush park with your dad in a world he created, sharing ideas, laughing about the past, cherishing each other's company. And all the while, your beloved dog is at your side, as she always was on earth.

You #7 — You do nothing. You simply bask in the endless sea of souls, buoyed by love, warmed by togetherness, cocooned by belonging.

You #8 — The year is 2216. Gone unchecked, climate change has ravaged the world, with rising water temperatures devastating the oceans' ecosystems. Tears streak your face as you watch the last whale on earth die of starvation. With you now existing in a world of endless love, this sorrow is so intense that it reverberates through all the other "yous."

You #9 — To cheer yourself up after the heartbreak of the whale, you quickly revisit your daughter's birth. The hospital room. The first time you held her. The first time she gazed into your eyes and you connected. Unbounded joy.

And there you have it. Just another day in the afterlife.

So, other than revisit cherished moments from your past, what can you do?

What can you imagine?

My Gift

A lot of what we've discussed has been supported with science and reasoned argument. Unfortunately, that doesn't make it all true. You see, at the risk of sounding like a skeptical scientist, there is no hard evidence to support the concepts we've explored here.

However, when you consider all the known facts that we do possess and combine those with the ideas that I'm proposing, the only logical way there could be an afterlife so that we get to do all the things we want to do is for it to work the way I've detailed.

You see, we don't live our lives guided by guarantees and safe scientific facts. Though you might imagine we do, we actually don't. We actually live our lives based on probability — the probability that if we drive to the store, we won't get mangled in a multicar crash; the probability that if we turn on the gas stove, it won't explode and we won't be incinerated in a great fireball, the probability that we'll wake up tomorrow and won't die in our sleep.

Probability governs our lives. And we're okay with that. And what is probability at heart? Faith. Whether you want to see that as faith in God, faith in humanity's achievements, or faith in our own abilities, it doesn't matter. It's faith. Period.

Now, you have to decide where the probability lies in everything I've shared with you. Do you have faith in my reasoning of what might constitute the afterlife, my logical deductions of what the soul is and how it interacts with the universe, my hypothesis of how all this so elegantly fits together?

And it *is* elegant.

The way all the pieces slot into place to create an amazing picture, like the most magnificent jigsaw puzzle you've ever seen — there's no other word for it but elegant. It all fits so perfectly, it's hard to believe the afterlife could be any other way, isn't it?

And that means one thing — you no longer need fear the end.

If you believe in this afterlife because it seems perfect, just the way the afterlife should — so perfect it couldn't possibly be any other way — then that is the end of the fear of losing a loved one, the end of the fear of dying, the end of the fear of not existing anymore.

Comfort.

Assurance.

Security.

Peace.

I hope those are my gifts to you.

Enjoy a long and happy life, my friend. And an even longer and even happier afterlife!

Questions about Heaven

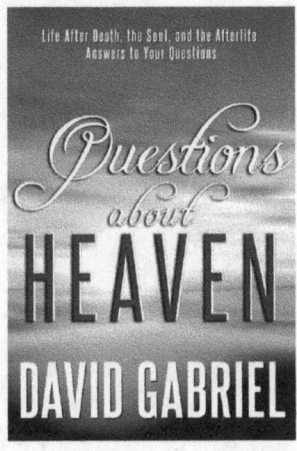

You and Heaven covered an immense amount of information, but there were a number of topics that were outside the scope of that book, so they are explored in great detail in *Questions about Heaven*, using a simple question and answer format. For example:
> Will it hurt when I die?
> Do my loved ones protect and watch over me?
> Does Hell exist?
> Are guardian angels real?
> If a child dies, do they grow up in heaven?
> How can I know I'm forgiven by someone I've lost?
> If I remarry, who do I meet in the afterlife?
> Is death scary?
> And many, many more.

Get *Questions about Heaven* today.